Power Presentation

As Director of Voice at London's Royal National Theatre and the Guildhall School of Music and Drama, Patsy Rodenburg, OBE is recognized as one of the world's leading voice and acting coaches. Patsy seamlessly transfers her coaching techniques from the stage into the realm of everyday life.

www.patsyrodenburg.com

- Z
- Wall
- Da Vinci
- bowling

Acknowledgements

With thanks to Kate Adams, Louise Bakker, Arabella Stein, Debbie Hatfield, Antonia Franceschi and to all the students at the Guidhall School of Music and Drama.

Power Presentation

Formal speech in an informal world

PATSY RODENBURG

MICHAEL JOSEPH
an imprint of
PENGUIN BOOKS

MICHAEL JOSEPH
Published by the Penguin Group
Penguin Books Ltd, 80 Strand, London WC2R 0RL, England
Penguin Group (USA) Inc., 375 Hudson Street, New York,
New York 10014, USA
Penguin Group (Canada), 90 Eglinton Avenue East, Suite 700, Toronto, Ontario,
Canada M4P 2Y3 (a division of Pearson Penguin Canada Inc.)
Penguin Ireland, 25 St Stephen's Green, Dublin 2, Ireland
(a division of Penguin Books Ltd)
Penguin Group (Australia), 250 Camberwell Road, Camberwell, Victoria 3124,
Australia (a division of Pearson Australia Group Pty Ltd)
Penguin Books India Pvt Ltd, 11 Community Centre, Panchsheel Park,
New Delhi – 110 017, India
Penguin Group (NZ), cnr Airborne and Rosedale Roads, Albany, Auckland 1310,
New Zealand (a division of Pearson New Zealand Ltd)
Penguin Books (South Africa) (Pty) Ltd, 24 Sturdee Avenue,
Rosebank, Johannesburg 2196, South Africa
Penguin Books Ltd, Registered Offices: 80 Strand,
London WC2R 0RL, England
www.penguin.com

First published 2009
1

Set in Galliard
Typeset by seagulls.net
Printed in Great Britain by Clays Ltd, St Ives plc

A CIP catalogue record for this book is available from the British Library

ISBN 978-0-718-15411-0

To Max Rodenburg, my father, with love

Contents

Introduction

On the morning of Wednesday 5th November, the day after the US presidential election, I arrived to teach at the Guildhall School of Music and Drama, elated, even though I had had no sleep. Inevitably my students wanted to talk about the momentous event that they were witnessing and as I am a teacher of voice and communications, we naturally discussed Barack Obama's speech and presentation.

I was with first-year students aged between 18 and 24 and as they spoke I was struck by – in hindsight – a blatantly obvious epiphany: the majority of these students had never heard a politician speak like Barack Obama. That is, a world leader speaking with **clarity**, **dignity**, **focus**, **passion**, **humanity** and **authenticity**. A man prepared to care through his presentation and content. A man desiring that his words inspire and awaken.

My young students hadn't heard Mandela – they have lived through politicians using spin to hide the truth, and smirking and mocking as a presentation style. They have only experienced the casual, cynical approach to communication; the approach that assumes the audience is not equal to the presenter and can be duped.

On that morning, I had real hope that these students had begun to understand the power of words and the power of presence.

This book will put power and presence into your own speech. You will realize that even if you don't perceive yourself as a leader, at the moment you present in any context you *are* leading and you have to own your power and authority. In classical moral philosophy, power and leadership are rigorously discussed. Quite simply, if you have power you must use it for the general good and use it responsibly. But – and here's the paradox – you *must* use it. Most communicators who fail have failed to realize they have power and that power has an impact on all around. It is your role to lead as you communicate and you are going to fail if you don't do it with presence.

It is probably safe to say that by picking up this book you know or believe that your ability to communicate is in some way failing you. You might have a fear or even a terror of speaking in public or an intense dislike of your voice. Perhaps your presentation has been criticized or even mocked, or you simply want to be better. When communication matters you are not as successful as your mind and heart want and know you can be. In other words, you know you are much more interesting than you sound!

I have spent my life working on voice, language and effective delivery. It is my passion and I only started this journey because of my own fears and struggles to communicate. I understand the pain and distress concerned with any inability you experience when your communication fails and I honour the struggle you face as you attempt to improve your voice and your verbal impact on the world.

However, you will soon realize that I intend to be direct and truthful as this book is for those of you who really want to work on and improve your presentation.

The work will demand practice and honesty, and in order to be a great communicator and presenter you will have to release your power, attention and presence. You have to accept certain non-negotiable truths.

Any communication that matters to you or the listener can never be casual or unprepared.

Communication is personal – human to human – and is at its best when there is humanity within the speaker.

Good communication, like achievement in any field, takes hard work, diligence and preparation.

Long before you breathe in and open your mouth to speak, even as you walk into a room or stand up to begin speaking, the people around you have made decisions as to whether they will lend you their ears or give you their respect.

- How comfortable do you look?

- No-one can listen to a boring voice for more than a couple of minutes.

- No-one wants to or enjoys listening to a pushed or aggressive voice.

- The extreme effort required in listening to a mumbled voice frustrates, and although the overbeautiful voice can enthral, that thrill is pointless if we hear the beauty of the voice rather than the words being spoken.

- No-one trusts arrogance, spin or apology.

- No-one wants to be addressed by a fidget or by someone so physically stiff that they can't move. Both positions exasperate us.

- No-one likes people who want to be liked, and those speakers who have a 'fuck you' attitude don't amuse us as they alienate goodwill.

- If you rush, we can't keep up; if you speak too slowly, we take offence as we think you think we are stupid.

- We don't want falseness — false power, charm or enthusiasm.

- We want the truth and we want your full attention.

- We want you to take full responsibility for what you say and stand by it.

We want you present. Presence in a speaker is the beginning and ending of all good and powerful communication.

This presence, which is a real and tangible energy, transforms all around it. When you communicate with your full presence your words will live, inspire, provoke and prevail.

Part 1

Power Presentation Preparation

1 The Three Circles of Energy in Power Presentation

The key to Power Presentation is human energy and how to maximize and use your present energy. I devised the Three Circles of Energy over thirty years ago as a clear description of how human energy works.

The First Circle is a human energy that is connected to itself. In First Circle you are preoccupied with yourself, you are probably in the past and in a place of taking and being unable to give.

The Third Circle is a generalized energy that comes from you and is blasted out into the world non-specifically. It is an energy of force and control. It is of the future. It is give and no take. In its worst manifestations, it means that people feel like objects rather than individuals.

When you are present you are in the Second Circle. Your energy is connected to a specific point outside you. It is a place of give and take. You are connected to yourself and the world around you. Your audience is not a general mass but made up of individuals, and an exchange of energy takes place between you. The Second Circle energy is intimate and epic. It is the energy of survival and compassion. It is powerful but not forceful. By working through this book, you will learn to appreciate and understand these paradoxes and enjoy them! All these energies manifest in your body, breath, voice, speech, mind, heart and ears. They are contagious and will transform your ability to communicate effectively in all situations.

This will not be a strange magical mystery tour but a reconnection with your knowledge and experience which you can harness and control to be more powerful and effective. Any moment of real curiosity and interest connects you to your presence. Any situation that requires survival will place you into your presence. When you are completely connected to something outside yourself – be it eye contact with a stranger across a crowded room or a beautiful painting – you are present. An unknown sound in the house at night or the startling connection you find with great music puts you into a listening presence. You will learn how to pragmatically channel your full presence and consequently your full power.

The Three Circles of Energy will transform your ability to communicate effectively in all situations and with work, the energy of Second Circle will become organic and constantly accessible, even in a time when human presence is under threat.

Let us begin before the real work on Second Circle, by examining the all-too-common First and Third Circle presentation energies.

First Circle Presentation

First Circle energy is when you focus energy on yourself. Your main point of concentration is internal. This energy is reflective and to the outside world you appear hidden or absent.

The physical signs of First Circle energy include a general slump or depression in your physical presence. You might walk scuffing your feet, or shuffle or fidget. Your head might droop forward slightly, resulting in very little eye contact with your audience. It often appears that you are more interested in the floor than the space around you. Shoulders can be rounded and the upper chest depressed with the spine being collapsed. And when standing in First Circle the feet are often too close together, the knees locked and weight back on the heels.

These tensions will communicate negatively to your audience long before you open your mouth and the communication will be ineffective as you appear weak, unsure and therefore unable to inspire confidence. Your breath and your voice will be affected and further disempower you as the chain reaction continues. The First Circle voice can be barely audible. It can sound strained or be whispered, and the vocal energy falls back into the speaker instead of reaching the audience. This gives the words a mumbled or swallowed quality and sentences drop off and fall into the ground. This voice will often sound pessimistic, tired or bored and makes you feel more self-conscious. And you can't be a good listener in First Circle. Your imploding energy closes you off into a bubble so you are disengaged and often miss the point or misinterpret the conversation.

From the moment you come forth to speak you are signalling, 'I don't want to be here, I don't trust what I am saying, I don't care about my material, I don't care about you, nothing matters.' Now it is very likely you don't feel or think these things at all, but it's what comes across.

There is a belief that microphones will save the First Circle speaker. Wrong.

A microphone only amplifies what is there. If you are mumbling we just hear a louder mumble. Many First Circle speakers have been wooed into believing that their low-esteem posture and fidgeting will be hidden by fantastic visuals. If that is the case then why be there at all? Show a movie! If you are there you have to *be* there.

Third Circle Presentation

It is normal that First Circle speakers rapidly realize that their energy habits are completely ineffective in any important communication. The habitual First Circle communicator is more likely to seek help or stop presenting and find another route to power by being completely brilliant in some specific subject or discipline. Not so with Third Circle presenters, for whom there is an easy trap to fall into when speaking. The trap is that on a superficial level, a Third Circle presentation can be effective. It can control an audience and pump generalized energy into a room. However, it rarely inspires or makes the audience believe they matter. Because the Third Circle speaker splays out their energy without any specific focus and although this energy can be enthusiastic, aggressive or entertaining it doesn't take the listener into consideration and is therefore controlling.

If First Circle energy is a place of denial, then Third Circle energy is one of bluff. This bluff can be seen in the bodies of Third Circle speakers. The chest is lifted and shoulders pulled back. The chin can be pulled up, giving the impression that we are being looked down upon, or the head thrust forward which overpenetrates our space. The jaw is often clenched with anticipation. When standing, the feet can be often too far apart, the walk too firm and noisy. The Third Circle body can invade others' space – space invaders who won't give way or yield to another body. They seem to take up too much space. This physical tension puts up a shield that desensitizes them to others.

A Third Circle voice is generally pushed and often too loud. We can always hear a Third Circle speaker but rarely listen. They are not listening to us – they do sometimes listen to themselves – which is why one of the most common habits of Third Circle is to interrupt or shout us down. They don't want your opinion unless it is their own.

You might have noticed that I didn't address you as a Third Circle speaker. The negative attributes of Third Circle are harsh and while I want you to recognize when you fall into this energy I don't want you to blame yourself. What's important is to realize that this type of presentation will get you through but it won't engage your audience or make a positive impact. It's a quick fix that just doesn't work in the long run.

Second Circle Presentation

When you are lucky enough to experience a present Second Circle presentation or meeting you will encounter some or even all of the following qualities.

- The speaker will have an energized yet open body and delivery.

- You will feel that you, the listener, matter, and through the speaker's eye contact you will feel connected to the presentation.

- You will feel spoken 'to' not 'at'.

- Their voice will be open and clear, not pushed and forcing you back.

- You won't have to struggle to hear them but will listen with ease.

- The speaker will have energy and passion but this energy appears effortless and efficient.

- You won't worry about the speaker as their presence makes you secure in the knowledge that they know what they are doing.

- There is authenticity and humanity in their presence and even if there are a thousand people present, the speaker is speaking to you alone.

These qualities are communicated because the speaker has focused their energy on you. There is no focus on themselves, or any general outward sweep of splayed energy. The focus is on specific points outside themselves – this energy is given to and takes from those points.

Form and Content

A great and inspiring communicator is present and in Second Circle contact with the form and content of their presentation. We will be discussing and working on both but at the beginning of this journey you should assess what you are good at.

Form is how you present through your body, voice and speech and if this is in Second Circle then you will be communicating physically very well. However, you could have been trained in form but have no connection or presence with content.

In other words, you might sound great but actually say nothing. Certain educations teach this extremely well: well-presented hollowness.

Or you could have great content and know and own your knowledge in Second Circle but struggle to form it through your physical acts of communication.

I have to say that if your content is good but your form poor, you have probably been frustratingly overlooked and enraged at the success of hollow presenters.

Perhaps it is a sign of the times but I am increasingly noticing that the hollow ones are crumbling and failing while those with content are moving into the forefront as leaders.

Let us harness both form and content in power presentation.

2 Tools of the Trade

The vast majority of us were born with an efficient and aligned body, a wonderful voice, remarkable speech muscles, a full and releasing breath system and ears that can hear clearly and precisely. These are the tools of your trade when it comes to Power Presentation but they are often made rusty with bad habits. It's time to strip those away and return you to that natural empowering state. Remember:

- Every part of your body, breath, voice, speech and listening abilities communicates consciously or unconsciously to an audience. If you feel trapped in your body or your voice then your message will be trapped.

- If the body is tense, then the breath and voice are tense. A tense voice constricts the sounds and generalizes the meaning. We can all hear a pushed voice but can't really distinguish the words.

- If you can't breathe fully you cannot voice, feel or think fully.

Unless you are fully present and care about what you are saying your body, breath, voice, speech and listening abilities won't work together and cannot really impact on the world. We have all seen beautifully placed bodies and heard resonant voices but unless they are present and the human being in them is actually *there* then we don't really care.

BODY

Your natural body, before it becomes warped and distorted by life, is an amazingly aligned, powerful and efficient embodiment of you and your presence. Watch a young child alert with curiosity and wonder. They stand or sit with their naturally good posture, shoulders released, head balanced, feet on the ground and their whole being focused forward on and into their point of concentration. Their bodies are clean of any useless tension.

You started there.

You have a memory of being completely and unselfconsciously in your body and you have to excavate and rediscover that body. Something and someone took that body away from you – a remark, a need to please or a need to be unnoticed in a room drove you to distort the very thing that houses you.

After good physical exertion, at the point of exhilaration (before exhaustion!), your body is present. Rowing, surfing, skateboarding, windsurfing, rock-climbing, a brisk walk over rough ground, martial arts, all place you in efficient alignment. In fact, any activity that can only be achieved by ignoring the useless grips of tension will return our often underused, decadent bodies to their natural presence.

If you have ever faced danger and coped rather than fallen to pieces, you might remember how all the useless tensions dropped off your body, enabling you to become fully present and consequently survive.

Begin to notice activities that place you into your body. This is the present, powerful Second Circle body that you must bring to every important meeting and communication.

Where Are You Now?

You have flashes of presence in your body but where are you now?

Do You Live Mostly in a First or Third Circle Body?

Gather recent photographs of yourself. Find some that you posed for and some that were taken surreptitiously and include some side and back shots of your body. Try to find photos in which you are not wearing heavy or concealing clothes. Stand and look at yourself in a full-length mirror. Even lingering in front of a reflective shop window will be very informative.

When you start looking at yourself in photos and mirrors you will begin to gather a goldmine of information that will immediately change you, the world around you and every act of communication you make from now on.

- Starting from the top of your body, begin to assess where and how you generally hold your head. Do you pull it back with your chin in the air or push it forward so it juts out (Third)? Do you look down, is it hard to see your eyes or do you hold your head to one side (First)? The head is very heavy and all of these positions place an inefficient work toll on your neck and spine, and affect your voice. From the audience point of view the Third Circle head positions signal superiority or acute determination if not aggression. The First Circle head positions signal shyness, a victim or submissiveness.

- Moving down, the state of your shoulders can, and I am not dramatizing this, destroy your ability to be effective. The shoulders should naturally hang without distortion, bracing or placing. We are designed to swing! You can't swing if the shoulders are held or placed. Any tension in your shoulders will have a direct impact on your ability to breathe, produce your voice, or speak freely. I believe that this tension is so powerful that when we see it in others our shoulders rise or tense with the speaker's. Over the years I have put hundreds of very fearful performers on stage and I can tell you without doubt that unless they can release their shoulders they have not a hope in dealing with their fear. That is how crucial it is to address your shoulder tensions. In First Circle the shoulders lift up or are pulled around. In Third Circle they are pulled back or forced down.

- Still in relation to your shoulders, now look more specifically at your chest, particularly your sternum, that plate of bone that protects your heart. With First Circle shoulders your chest has collapsed. Viewing from the side you can see your chest is depressed and from the back you are rounded so, in effect, you are hidden and this is what comes across to your audience. With Third Circle shoulders your sternum has lifted itself up and pushes your chest into the world. From the side you are hoisted up into space through the sternum and from the back you can see the back locked around mid-centre. This braced and hoisted chest might feel strong to you but actually is weakening your breath and spine. You are shielding you heart, and we the audience feel that you are unreachable and untouchable. This position is the antithesis of being open and vulnerable — both essential qualities in the give and take of being present and in the dialogue of life. You might appear forceful but not powerful. Power has vulnerability and sensitivity! You are dangerous to others and yourself without these qualities.

The placing of the sternum is connected to the state of your spine. Many years ago I knew a genius osteopath, who had worked with the great Alexander. He said quite simply, 'Patsy, when your spine goes, you age.' You can do all the cosmetic surgery you want but if the spine has no real placing or strength you will age rapidly. Today I see young people with the spines of pensioners. Unnatural head positioning, shoulder and sternum tensions will contribute to debilitating back pain but more directly if your spine is slumped or held too rigidly the centre of your body and being will crumble. You cannot be in your body and breathe fully and are consequently, to the world, a pushover.

- Look at your spine. Is it slumped? This collapse of a slumped spine can be seen from the front around the centre of the body, pushing the stomach out and pulling the head down. From the side the back rounds in and the shoulders curve round. From behind you are ball-shaped. This physical stance screams 'spineless' to the world. It is the classic First Circle victim posture.

  Is your spine too rigid, held in place without any give or flexibility? So many of us have been taught to sit up straight and pull our shoulders back as a quick way to improve the adolescent slump. Although the spine looks strong when held in this way, its lack of flexibility constricts the neck, jaw, shoulders, upper chest and stomach muscles. Without freedom in the spine you are also a 'push over'. Stand braced and in this way and you can be floored with a shove. The weakness in this Third Circle posture lies in its lack of give and flexibility.

It is a forced stance rather than a powerful one. If you present with this spine the lack of give in it communicates a sureness bordering on stubbornness, an unchallengeable quality for people who are easily intimidated but for those who enjoy a challenge it beckons an attack. The lack of give in this kind of spine can even make you seem like a bully or someone intolerant of transformation. A tree with this kind of rigidity would not survive a storm.

- Now look at your abdominal area, the stomach and the whole pelvic area. As you move further from your head and where your voice is produced – the larynx in the neck – it is easy to believe that these areas do not matter to your ability to present, particularly if you do most of your work sitting down. This assumption comes directly from a society that has forgotten we are not heads on sticks but physical beings that have to breathe and feel fully in order to think and live fully.

Other complex issues around this abdominal area are twinned with vanity and sex. Holding in the stomach is a device most of us have tried to appear slimmer and wriggling or thrusting out the pelvic area are habits used to display sexual interest.

The full power of the human breath system is stored in this area. You could even say our whole human power is centred here. I can prove that the breath-support muscles of the abdominal muscles power the voice's full release. I cannot prove but I strongly suspect that all our deep and profound feelings lodge here. Here lives your authentic self, and here is produced your authentic voice.

Holding or distorting the abdominal area severely impedes your ability to speak fully – particularly to large groups of people – and blocks your emotional connections as you speak. You cannot be passionate. You can't fully feel and therefore your audience cannot feel you or what you say. You have no power and you are disconnected from your presence.

Look at your abdominal area. If you can see a hold you will also be able to feel it. As we have discussed, everything in the body is interconnected. So, if our spine is slumped, the stomach is squashed out. If you have that habit it might seem appropriate to pull your stomach in to flatten it rather than reposition your spine.

Do you push your pelvic area forward? This position can best be identified by looking at yourself sideways. The effect of this pelvic thrust is actually making your upper body lean back. You will also notice that your heavy head is having to be held into place by, probably, very distressed neck muscles – a real cause of neck- and headaches.

Stomach holders and pelvic thrusters appear in both First and Third Circle bodies. Generally in First the holds are there to diminish power. In Third it is an attempt to force their presence and at worst can seem preening or a sexual come-on.

Whatever the reason, as you walk into a room these holds communicate a self-awareness – a pelvic thrust is pulling your back in so that your body looks like you don't want to be there. These tensions can be so extreme that you actually look like you are moving backwards although you are walking forwards. This clearly communicates: 'I don't want to be walking into this space.'

● The next section of the body is in three parts: legs, knees and feet. Over the last few years I, and many others who work on bodies, have noticed an alarming disconnection through the legs and feet. It is partly because we are so sedentary, and if we do walk, it is often on hard flat surfaces that pound the body, instead of rough ground — which is how our legs, knees and feet have evolved. I have increasingly noticed a split-screen effect in younger bodies. That is, the upper body might be engaged but the lower part is withering and shuffling around.

To be strong, present and engaged you have to stand fully on your legs and have your feet on the ground. Even when sitting, you must have your feet on the ground. Next time you see someone fidget, sway or shuffle in front of you, look at their feet, they won't be grounded. We all need the earth under our bodies and that comes up through the feet, calves, knees and thighs, into the hips.

Look at your legs, knees and feet. Can you feel your legs? Can you feel your feet on the floor? If you can't then they have been so wrongly placed that they are almost redundant. When you stand are your feet close together (First)? If your feet are wide — outside the width of your hips — then you are taking up more space than you need and is efficient for you (Third).

Are your knees locked back? The multiple effects and tensions of locked knees include tight abdominal muscles, impeded breath, tightening of the spine and tension in the neck and larynx. There is evidence that much knee surgery is related to the backward locking of the knees. Of course the knees are not designed to be locked in this way; you can't walk, run or move over any natural terrain with locked knees.

As soon as you lock your knees the whole body braces and there is no possibility of a rapid or fluid response through your being, either physically, emotionally or intellectually. Generally people who visibly shake when presenting in public are knee lockers. The locked knees create a block so that fear and stress are stuck in the body, and the pressure that creates ends up shattering the block, manifested by shaking. It is the same principle as building flexible buildings in earthquake zones. If a building has no give it crumbles! The bracing of the knees can effectively withdraw the body into First or be an attempt to stand firmly in Third.

While you are examining your knees, have a good look at your thighs as there will be subtle clues there. Thighs that are clamped together indicate a First Circle body. This clamp closes down the whole of the lower body and stops any breath going into the lower support muscles. If the thighs are turned out they might be trying to signal availability and strength but like most Third Circle habits they are weakening you as you are not fully standing on your legs. Notice, too, that the knees and thighs are connected to the flexibility of the ankles. Soften the ankles and the legs feel better.

Now really look at and feel where your feet are. I will only half sing a favourite aria of many body experts but you should at this point hear an excerpt of this aria. Thousands and thousands of bodies are ruined by shoes that are ill-fitting or stylish but are destroying the natural alignment of the body. This starts in childhood and I suppose was brought to its highest conclusion in the Chinese practice of foot-binding. If you cannot run away in your shoes and on your feet you are displaying the epitome of powerlessness. I should also say that many training shoes are designed for running and not standing because when you stand they can pull your whole body back into First Circle stance.

Rest assured when you learn about your body and how it should be working you can wear whatever shoes you want, and although to stay present and in your Second Circle body will take a bit more concentration and physical compensations, you will be able to present in the latest style of knock-'em-out shoes.

Enough of fashion. Take off your shoes. Stand and look down at your feet.

Are you standing more on one foot? Are you standing back on your heels or on the side of your feet? Do your feet want to shuffle? Are they close together or splayed out? All these habits will tend to pull you into First. The only Third Circle feet habits that are easily spotted are feet that are too far apart or ones that actually grip the floor through their toes.

● The last look at the body is to explore how you habitually walk and sit.

Take a walk around the room. Walk until you feel you reach a comfortable stride.

Is your tendency to over-stride, often accompanied by the sound or feel of your feet on the ground? Do you push forward in your chest and chin, and swing your arms with vigour? Then you are a Third Circle walker! Do you walk with smaller strides than you need with the feet scuffing or scraping the floor? Do you look down to walk and pull your shoulders and spine into the ground? These habits suggest a First Circle walk.

Now look at yourself sitting. Do you feel a need to pull yourself up into a rigid sitting position with the chest braced? By now you will realize this is Third Circle and any slumping or falling back sitting puts you into First.

Body Tensions

Already you know a lot about the tensions that inhabit your body and where they distort you and pull you out of your presence. In spending a few minutes sensing and observing your own tensions you are beginning to have power over them.

Any tension that you have discovered in the relatively stress-free zone of your private work space or home can be trebled when that tension meets a burst of adrenalin or a shot of fear. Whatever tension you have discovered, however small, will matter when communication matters.

As you work further on your body, you will begin to focus in on what I term your 'primary tensions'. These are the tensions that trigger a domino effect throughout your body. Once the primary tension is identified you have an enormous ally. You begin to know your enemy: the enemy locked in your body. It is quite possible that this tension might haunt you for years but knowing it is there will give you a moment-by-moment chance to work it out of your body and presentation and return yourself to your full power.

The trouble with primary tensions is they tend to be hidden under their more obvious secondary ones. This results in people often saying to me, 'My shoulders are tight, I release them but they never get any better.' Generally the shoulders are a secondary tension triggered by spine, pelvic or knee tensions. These strange physical distortion scenarios get much worse when your body surges with energy that is trying to place you and your body in Second Circle presence.

Begin to identify your primary tension and how this tension can ripple out of its primary source to infect other parts of your body and destabilize your power. This exploration can take time so don't worry if you can't identify sources of distortion immediately.

The next stage is to understand how the energy of Second Circle presence, be it the energy of survival, fear, excitement, standing up in front of an audience or being the messenger of ill-tidings, can constrict you more than your everyday habits. Quite simply, if your body is not free then the great surges of the energy which is your life force can, and probably will, disable you more. As you lose your presence more and more, finding it in the body and breath can feel shocking. This energy surge through a distorted body is one of the reasons panic attacks grip so many people today. The heavily corseted Victorian upper-class women give us a vivid display of this. When passions or presence wanted to flow through them they couldn't. These women couldn't breathe so they fainted instead. The corset is, of course, a man-made physical distortion.

Identifying Primary Tensions

Here are some distortions I have regularly encountered. Every-one is different so the exact nature of each distortion is ultimately infinite but I think you will get the picture.

Let's start with a habitual First Circle body. You might notice that your shoulders are rounded and your head pulled down. You might even have tried to right the shoulders by pulling them back, actually increasing the distortion. The primary tension could be in the spine or even the knees. Until you address the key tension you will feel and look like a contortionist.

When you feel a surge of energy move through you the blocks might force your First Circle body into Third Circle with your chest lifting up, making it almost impossible to breathe. This can lead to your voice shooting up in pitch and losing any real power.

You might be feeling your main source of tension in your neck or lower back and feel your shoulders uplifted most of the time. The primary tension here could be in a hard pelvic area with the stomach muscles pulled in.

As the energy surge runs through you, you might feel pushed back as though your presence makes you retreat. Many First Circle bodies are not on their legs but are existing with locked knees and no decent grounding through the feet. When this occurs, the whole upper body is fighting to stay upright and tensions lock in through the spine, stomach, upper chest, shoulders and neck. The whole upper body has no foundation so that when filled with an energy surge the whole body implodes and crumbles.

The Third Circle body is completely prone to pushing itself out into the world and being inflexible. Many Third Circle bodies complain of lower back pain and tension but actually the primary tension is in the upper chest which has been pulled up and out. In these cases when an energy surge occurs the chest gets so locked that you can find yourself hyperventilating and even shaking.

Another tension that can be keenly felt in Third is one in the throat that can tighten the voice. However, the primary tension can be the shoulders being locked back and held into place. With this combination of tensions the voice has no chance to work freely and you will end up pushing or even losing it or feeling very hoarse after a big presentation.

As a Third Circle body you will begin to rapidly recognize the puffed-up tension of the torso but you must also realize your primary tension could be in the locked stance of your legs. The upper torso is responding to a lack of real connection through the legs and feet to the ground. I completely understand that you interpret this as strength, but in fact, with a sufficient surge of energy you will prove brittle and may shatter.

Returning to the Whole

Now begins the work that will re-place your body into its natural state, its state of power, its place as a vessel for all your energy to pass through you without constriction.

Throughout the book I include exercises that seem to work best for the majority of the people, but I know from years of experience that not all exercises work for every single person. Give each exercise a go with goodwill and if it doesn't change you at all dispose of it and try another. These exercises have been designed in a particular order and remember when an exercise works, you might need it for the rest of your life. Some of these exercises do need time and privacy but others can be done quickly throughout the day. Like all good practice and craft training, an exercise has to change you organically so that you know the exercise so well that you can forget it! For this to happen it is better that you exercise a bit each day rather than, say, two hours once a week, and you must be prepared to check in with any problem several times a day. I know this can be difficult in a hectic lifestyle but you do deserve time for yourself, even if you have to work secretly away from colleagues. I work with a top politician who checks out all problems in the toilet away from prying eyes. Once you are familiar with the basic exercises there are quick reminders at the back of the book.

Deep Floor Release

This exercise can change your life. It is designed to place your body naturally in its full efficient alignment. It will also help to alleviate stress and aids deep relaxation into sleep. Use this exercise to clear yourself of daily stress and negative physical intrusions into your body. It takes time and you need a secure and safe place to do the full release. You can't do this exercise and then get up and be immediately alert and effective. It can also be emotional. Many people find that they contact a whole series of forgotten feelings from rage to grief to loss. This is partly due to the breath settling in the lower abdomen. More of that later but don't be alarmed if you contact more feelings than you knew you had.

The essence of this exercise is to allow the gentle but relentless force of gravity to re-place your body. To release you of all those years of debilitating tensions.

The mainstay of the exercise is to lie on the floor with your calf muscles supported by a chair. Find a chair that comfortably supports your calf muscles without contortion so that your thighs can be at right angles to the floor. Experiment with chairs until you find one that is the right height for the length of your thigh muscles and enables you to lie at ease on the floor without any holds in your legs. In an ideal circumstance the thighs should be fully supported by the calf muscles on the chair.

- Find a safe, warm place where you won't be disturbed.

- Have a thin cushion to hand in case you need it to support your head.

- Lie on your back and place the chair so it can support your calf muscles. Make sure you are straight along the floor and if you feel your head is falling back so that your throat feels tight, place the cushion under your head so that the throat feels open. Move the head gently from side to side until it rests with ease. You are now looking up to the ceiling or sky.

- Release your jaw. Your lips should be together and your teeth unclenched.

- Let your shoulders open. Your arms, by your side, should feel heavy, as though they are sinking into the ground.

- Place your concentration on your sternum and see if you can still it so that it doesn't lift as you breathe. You might need to place a hand there to monitor any useless hoisting you might want to do.

- Feel the spine expand across the floor. There will be a section of the spine that doesn't touch the ground but you should feel an expansion across the upper back which allows the ground to support more of you.

- Now place your concentration on the release around your thighs. This release should begin to open your pelvic area and open locked stomach muscles.

To be fully effective you need to be in this position for a minimum of ten minutes and if the exercise works for you I will add other points of concentration until you are doing this for 20 to 30 minutes, three times a week. This is a deep release and relaxation exercise but there are many common misconceptions around words like 'release' and 'relaxation'. This exercise can, initially, be uncomfortable. Release generally aches. If you are holding tensions in your body you will ache as the body releases and finds its natural position. These tensions are habits that might have been locked into your body for decades. Your neck, shoulders, upper chest, lower back and stomach could ache.

Every time you do this exercise try to allow the body to spread out and your weight to be taken by the earth. It will get better each time you do it and very importantly you will begin vividly to identify tensions and new traumas that have entered the body. This exercise will not only be a wonderful rediscovery of yourself every time you do it but will give you a clear warning of any impeding physical problems.

After ten minutes (or longer when you progress) return to standing carefully and in a placed way:

- Roll over on to your side.

- Your legs will have come off the chair and you are lying on your side like a beached whale.

- Stay on your side until you feel your weight has been taken by the floor in that position.

- Now roll on to your hands and knees and slowly come up.

- Get your feet on the ground and roll up through the spine, letting your head come up last of all.

- Let the shoulders fall into place – where they want to go, not where you want to place them. They should feel heavy and open.

- Lift your spine into place by remembering how it felt on the floor. On the floor it wasn't rigid and arched nor could it be slumped.

- Do the same process with the pelvic area.

- Notice that the knees aren't locked.

- If you have a full-length mirror, go and look at yourself and see if you can see a different alignment.

- Now allow your head to fall on your chest and feel its weight.

- Let your weight flop the body over until the torso is hanging freely from the waist.

- Shake the shoulders and allow the back of the neck and jaw to release.

- Slowly roll up again and see if the placing is different, the shoulders released and the spine up.

This release and relaxation can place your mind and being into First Circle. You might find you have gone back into yourself and your body. The heels take the weight of your body and your chest may be slightly sunken. This is easily addressed:

- Look around the room and try to focus your energy on something outside yourself, like a picture or a tree through the window. This focused attention might pull your energy forward into Second.

- Next, walk with energy. Imagine you have somewhere to go and are moving directly but without force. As you walk in this way you will feel a new energy engage in you. There will be a gear change in your physical state.

- When you feel this shift stop walking but allow your body to keep moving forward. What I mean by that is stay on the balls of your feet and don't move back or settle by either locking your knees, pulling down or bracing up in your spine or interfering in the placing of your shoulders.

Do this walking exercise enough and you will start to be present in your body in an exciting way. This is how you should walk into any high-powered meeting. In fact, I have trained many leaders to practise this walk in their office before an important meeting. Let me be very specific – you cannot expect your presence to be powerful if you begin a presentation from a slumped physical stance. After one session a CEO emailed me: 'How did I even think I could be powerful when I was so physically casual?'

- Now go to a wall and place both hands on it as though you were going to gently but firmly push the wall over. Notice the contact you need throughout the body for this sensation of full power in the push to happen. Your feet have to be on the ground with the weight on the balls, the knees unlocked, the spine up, strong, but not rigid, the shoulders released so that you can feel the energy and breath low in the pelvic area.

- Breathe in this position. Stay connected to the wall, don't feel you are pulling the wall's energy into you or that you are forcing your upper body's power into the wall, just push with strong but efficient energy.

- When you feel this energy, move away from the wall, allowing the contact with the wall to place you into the room with your full physical presence. Again, this is the first impression that you should bring into any important meeting. You are beginning to allow your natural charisma to radiate from your body.

There is a knowledge in the theatre that if you come on stage with this power the audience will be with you from your first entrance. Then you can do anything. If you enter in First or Third then you have a battle on your hands to win them over (First) or to move them to care (Third).

Return to this deep release whenever stressed. Even two or three minutes in this position will help you thaw useless physical tensions after any stressful event, but do remember the longer version of this exercise might not be appropriate if you need to draw on powerful energy within the following hour. It is an excellent exercise for the evening before a presentation or important meeting.

Releasing and Positioning the Spine

You probably already know if your spine is problematic but this simple sitting exercise will give you clearer insights into the exact nature of the problem.

- Find a hard seat.

- Sit with both feet on the ground, applying a little extra pressure on the balls of your feet.

- Gently rock until you feel connected to the base of your spine.

- Keep the sense of the fluidity of the rock when you come to stillness.

- Now place your mind into the structure of your spine. Is it slumped in the middle or held rigidly there?

- Move the spine slowly and subtly up and down.

- You will begin to feel the moment when the spine finds its natural, balanced place.

- Recognize the spine's connection and influence on the sternum and shoulders. When the spine is in its natural position you will feel the chest is open, not lifted or depressed. The shoulders will begin to hang freely and correctly without you having to position or control them.

- Now stand up. You should have a greater sense of your spine and that sensation should go through your legs and knees into the ground.

Tip your weight an iota forward on to the balls of your feet and do this next spine exercise.

- Keep your knees soft and ankles supple and swing your arms up above you, as though you are reaching for the sky.

- Avoid lifting your shoulders or chest and keep the back of your neck loose.

- As you reach up, breathe to the sky and slowly open your arms to your side so that you present the balanced man image that Leonardo da Vinci drew.

- This is an important moment and your response here is crucial to all the exercises that follow. As your arms open to the world and then return to their place hanging by your side you must try to keep your spine up in the position the exercise has placed it in.

All through this work there is a simple instruction. Do the exercise and after its release try and remain in the place the exercise has put you in.

The 'Da Vinci' exercise can be repeated again and again and with this repetition you will begin to feel where your spine should naturally be.

This is one of the exercises done by the politician in the privacy of the toilet. Apparently he does this before any known encounters with a particularly powerful enemy. By finding his spine he does not feel so spineless in the enemy's presence.

As your spine finds its true position, don't be alarmed if muscles around the spine ache. This ache is not a spasm or a sharp pain but an ache of muscles suddenly working after years of retirement.

Go back to the pushing the wall exercise and as you do the push, feel the importance and power of the spine. A good variation of the wall exercise is to hold a chair above your head.

You might have already realized that a lot of my exercises actually trick the body and breath into finding their natural power and presence and these tricks will continue. If you hold a reasonably weighted chair above your head (find a chair that is not too heavy but with enough weight to place your body), the weight of the chair will centre your whole body in its need to hold up the chair. The proof of this exercise can be shown if, as you hold the chair, you play with the useless tensions many of us carry. They automatically relax. For instance, if you lock the knees you will feel an enormous and unhelpful reaction throughout the body that informs you of the inefficiency of locked knees.

The same is true with tension in the shoulders, as the placement of the spine and upper chest will signal the same inefficiency. When you manage to hold the chair high enough to adjust and centre the body, you will find a strong, upright, physical presence. At the point of feeling your centre, put the chair back on to the floor and relish your powerful, physical uprightness.

Shoulders

Most of us feel stress, fear and disempowerment in our shoulders. When the energy surge hits the shoulders they both rise, and because of the enforced tensions your breathing and voice can be affected.

- Gently move and circle your shoulders around. Don't be alarmed if they creak or crack; this is an indication that tension is releasing. After this movement let them find their own place. **Don't place them**.

- Now take a solid stance: one foot ahead of the other with the spine up and knees unlocked.

- Swing one arm around as though you are throwing a ball underarm.

- Don't try to do this aerobically but with focused ease.

- Maybe place your attention in Second Circle at a point or target ahead of you. You are throwing energy to that point.

- Remember to breathe.

- After several throws, let the arm and shoulder come to rest.

- If you resist placing the shoulder, you will allow it to find its natural and unstressed position. Generally this is much lower than the unreleased shoulders.

- Release the other shoulder and swing its arm and just appreciate how easy the shoulder can feel on the release when you don't interfere with it.

- Try swinging both arms round and let them find their true and natural place.

I fully understand that you can't prepare for a public presentation by overt releases of tension. The following two releases are more subtle.

- Stand with your feet under your hips and weight slightly forward on the balls of your feet.

- Keep the spine up and grasp your hands behind your back.

- Lift your arms up and away from your torso, and down to your body several times.

31

- When you unclench your hands the shoulders should release and find their natural position.

When you understand the release of this exercise you can do it once and reconnect your body by releasing the shoulder constriction that is impeding your full power.

The most subtle release you can do is very small and is reliant on you understanding the whole mechanism of your shoulder tensions. So this exercise might only work for you after a few months of work.

- Lift up the shoulders half an inch. Tense them there and then let them go and release.

What you will notice is that if they are riddled with tension, that tension will go.

The glory of this release is that you can do it without anyone noticing and you can regain control of your presence in the middle of any distressing and fearful encounter.

The true professional communicator knows that when tensions attack, all is not lost but can be regained with focused action. And that often means releasing the shoulders!

Release your shoulders before any important meeting so that you start freely and release them afterwards, so any tensions formed in the meeting are not carried through the rest of the day. Leave your desk and computer and release several times a day, even when not under threat. You will feel better and look better. One CEO tells me that his tailor is delighted with his shoulders as his bespoke suits hang on him with more style!

Pelvic Area

When you have pushed against a wall or held a chair above your head you will have already sensed the importance of your pelvic area being under your upper torso yet connected to your legs and feet. It is a bridge between the lower and higher parts of your body. Holding a chair above your head you will feel the weakness of pushing the pelvis forward as this will encourage your body to topple backwards or, if your tendency is to push your pelvic area and bottom backwards, you will begin to fall forwards with the chair. If you can hold the chair long enough with your shoulders free, the spine up and knees unlocked, the pelvic region will find its true place.

Equally, on the floor in the deep release position, gravity works its magic and opens and positions your centre power around this abdominal area.

A less dramatic but more subtle awareness of the pelvic position can be experienced in this way:

- Stand with your feet under your hips and hip-width apart. Make sure your feet are parallel – not turned in or out – and the weight of the body is felt in the balls of the feet. Keep the knees slightly bent.

- Let the head fall on to the chest and its weight flop you over from the waist. The neck should be free so that the head can move like a pendulum. The shoulders should hang.

- When you are hanging from the waist, allow the body's tensions to fall out of you.

- Start to come up through the spine and aim for the shoulders to fall into place and the head to be the last thing to come up, but place your real attention on the pelvic area. As you come up there is going to be a critical moment – normally when you are two thirds of the way up – when you might want to either push your pelvis forward or clench your buttocks. Both options lock your power and take you out of your presence.

You might have to do this exercise many times before you can allow the pelvis to be under your torso and a part of you. It is common for you to feel shaky as you reposition this area but the benefits you will experience – especially in the breath – will far outweigh the shakiness.

Head, Neck and Jaw

When you realize that the neck protects the crucial spinal chord as it enters the brain it is no wonder that any tension here heightens the stress and pain of life. 'A pain in the neck' is an appropriate cliché. Moreover, given the weight of the head, it is no wonder that if the head is not properly balanced at the top of the spine, then the whole voice and body can and will move towards trauma. The jaw is equally crucial. In my experience, jaw tension is the last to go and the first tension to return.

- Stand centred with all the connections you have found throughout your body.

- Stay present through feet, knees, spine and shoulders.

- Allow the head to drop on to your chest.

- Take both hands and gently massage the back of the neck and then move into the jaw and face.

- After a few minutes of this gentle massage, let the arms and shoulders return with gravity to your side.

34

- Gently swing your head from one side to the other.

- Do this at least seven times and then allow your head to rest again on the chest.

- Shut your eyes and lift your head.

- Don't open your eyes until you can feel your head balance easily on top of the spine.

- During this process you might find it useful to pivot the head around. The head is at the end of the spine so you must sense how important it is to have your spine straight. The importance of having your eyes closed is that you will begin to feel the head's real position rather than placing it according to visual clues.

- Place one hand gently on the front of your throat and see if that area feels more open. When you adopt your habitual head positions you should feel neck and throat constrictions.

- Now let the head fall to the right side.

- Keep the jaw released.

- Take the right arm and gently but firmly pull the head over a little, feeling a gentle stretch.

- Then let the arm drop and use it to pull down on the left, hanging arm.

- After a few seconds let go and allow the head to return upright.

- The left neck muscles will feel light and easy and the head position more balanced.

- Repeat on the other side.

- Suddenly the head position will feel wonderful. As the neck frees you will sense energy around you and begin · to have 'eyes in the back of your head'.

So many of the people I work with feel attached from behind – the 'knife in the back' scenario. This suspicion encourages many to close down the sensations in the neck and shoulders, which desensitizes the attack. However, when you are free in these areas, and present, you are aware of any plotting, which is the only safe place to be in.

The last body release is to address jaw and facial tensions. Many of us hold our faces in a mask of tension, be it oversmiling, a grim and frozen face or one that conveys a perpetual state of worry or even arrogance. Maybe you have noticed in yourself or others that these facial tensions stop us seeing the real and present person. Sometimes you can even observe in some people's eyes a startled and frightened gaze reaching through their mask. These tensions in the facial mask make it hard to see someone's humanity and authenticity, or even to trust the face. Obviously this lack of connection through the face with an audience is not conducive to powerful communication but there is another pressing concern with jaw and facial tensions.

If you don't release the jaw and face, it is harder to speak clearly. The muscles of articulation are impeded. There are three main holds in the face.

1. Between the eyes
2. Taut cheek muscles
3. The jaw – and tension in the jaw is so invasive that it can disturb the breath, tighten the voice and even inhibit hearing.

Try the following exercise to release these holds:

- Stand centred, releasing any body tensions you can feel.

- Bunch up the face, trying to isolate those muscles and keeping the tension only in the face.

- After a few seconds release the muscles, allowing them to find their own place on your skull. That is, don't replace the tension.

- It can be a strange feeling as the muscles find where they want to be.

- Breathe and appreciate this new facial freedom. If you look into a mirror after this release you might even see yourself better and more clearly.

- Now the position of your jaw is moving towards its proper position, lips together but the teeth unclenched.

- Lastly try this. Smile gently but fully. At first keep your lips together.

- Then, slowly, open your mouth but with the lift of the smile in place.

- Get the mouth open as far as it can go without force.

- Breathe in this position and you will feel the throat open and energy enter the body.

- You might even feel this movement of breath and energy into your lower abdominal area.

- Now join the lips back together without replacing any of the old tensions or clenching the teeth.

- The whole facial mask will have started to release and another look into a mirror will show a different you.

The jaw is a very susceptible area of tension and needs constant work to keep it free.

It is possible that the jaw's release can be very emotional and it can also shake with release but the benefits to you, your voice and speech, as well as how you appear in the world are so apparent that you must let this tension go.

A brilliant young woman – the only woman in an all-male office – discovered through these exercises that she smiled her way through the day. Not a smile of joy but one of a desperate 'like me' mask. The painful realization was that this panicked smile only made the men attack her more. These attacks subsided as her face released.

The best way to stay present in your body is to use it as designed. Activities that require balance and centredness are obvious choices in keeping Second Circle fitness. One of the safest and most effective ways of staying connected in your body is to walk with purpose, not an amble, over rough ground or on sand. As you do this, notice the world around you in precise detail. Within minutes you will be more present in your body. Stop every now and then and notice how the energy moves in you and around you even when you are still. You are still but are still active.

You can recreate this energy in a room. Bare boards are better than carpet but you can feel shifts in the body on any surface.

- Walk with purpose and change direction cleanly. Notice the room around you and don't look at the floor.

- Every now and then stand still but don't pull away into First or pull up into Third within yourself or the space.

- Try sitting and then standing with this energy.

To feel Second Circle presence more vividly, run into walking into standing into sitting. Then reverse the journey. The repetition of this sequence will give you enormous power and presence when you walk into any room, sit down, then stand up to speak. It will give you a memory of how to switch on the energy and control it for your own success. I once spent an hour teaching a group of young MPs to stand up with presence in order to be noticed by the House of Commons speaker. Up to that point, none of them had managed to be noticed. All we did for an hour was practise standing and sitting with energy. After this session, within a week, they had all been able to be noticed and ask a question in the House of Commons. You can watch any great performer do the same. As they walk on stage, long before they speak or sing or pick up their instrument to play, you know they are there with you and present. They cannot be ignored (First) but are not intruding (Third) until it is their turn to do so.

Summary

- Pay attention to your posture – head, spine, shoulders, abdomen and legs. Make sure everything is in alignment and free of tension

- Pay attention to your face – relax your jaw, your forehead and your cheeks

- Stay connected to your body by staying present and mindful of your physicality

BREATH

Your whole life force, thoughts, feelings and expressions are completely reliant on oxygen and your ability to breathe. As life places you in heightened and important arenas you need your natural and present breath system more and more.

There is a simple equation in communication.

The bigger the thought, feeling and space = the more urgent the message = the greater the breath

You were born with a powerful and adaptable respiratory system. If you stop interfering with the breath it works very efficiently. By interference I mean tensions in the shoulders, chest or abdominal area, holds, gasps, sighs or the blocks you place on yourself emotionally and intellectually.

A natural breath responds to any new event, be it speaking in public, surviving an attack, a surge of an idea or an emotion. The natural breath allows the ribcage to open around the centre of the body, which by now you know is impossible to do fully if you are tense in the spine, shoulder, chest or jaw areas. This movement of breath inspiration then moves low into the body and opens up and releases all the lower abdominal muscles. As you breathe out, this energy sends your power into the world, through your voice, your words or your presence.

The breath deep in your body gives you power to act, speak, think and feel, and this action creates a column of air that supports you. This breath is what you need to be effective in all parts of your life. Sadly, most people live on a half-breath and therefore are not living presently or fully.

After any big event you should return your breath pattern and rhythm to one of ease so that the stress is breathed out of you. Every parent knows this sensation. When you comfort a child after its anxiety, you wait for the settling of the breath before you place the baby back into its bed. Somewhere in your history you will remember this glorious and liberating breath. It might be immediately recalled in the abandonment of a free laugh with your sides and stomach aching with the release of your breath's full and natural power.

Although many will feel those free breath moments are rare, they can be found again. Fortunately, breathing is a vital life function that can be consciously worked and sustained. This is essential if you are going to navigate yourself through fear and stress. Fear and stress will always be factors in important communication but they don't need to make your breath system explode (Third) or implode (First) with life's pressures. Remember, a trained actor or performer goes on stage with enormous stress but the performer's breath craft doesn't allow the stress to show, or the fear in the breath to destroy their work. They have consciously worked their breath systems to eliminate any impact fear has on their ability to breathe.

Start to think about your breath patterns. You will have to build up this awareness over a substantial period of time. The most interesting moments will be when you are under some form of threat; then you will discover your key breath tensions and begin to know how to face them. You have already received a lot of information about your breath through the body work and you probably have a strong suspicion as to your favourite circle. Here is how the three circles of energy manifest themselves in our breathing.

First Circle Breath

The extreme First Circle habit is for the pause between breaths to be overlong. In effect this collapses you into the smallest space you can occupy and you are attempting to become still and unnoticed if not invisible. Mice do this when a hawk hovers over them. It is a way of surviving that moment of extreme threat but the mouse will start to fully breathe again when the danger is over. It needs oxygen to scamper away. Some of you have been so terrorized that you are the still and inactive mouse but have forgotten to breathe when out of danger.

If you have this 'mouse syndrome' you might find yourself having to take a large and tense intake of oxygen after long intervals of not breathing properly. First Circle breathing has an irregular quality to it. There are gasps, quick top-ups of breath in the upper chest, sighs that weaken your power, deflating your body more. There is often a movement in the breath from a place of panic to one of resignation. All these habits are completely useless in powering the voice and can frighten your own voice so much that the pitch of the voice goes up to squeaks and whines. The irregular and rushed rhythm of breath signals weakness and it is my belief that this pattern communicates to the world that you are a victim. In my experience, bullies sense this pattern. In the presence of any bully you will feel this breath panic and will have to start breathing naturally through their presence in order to keep yours.

Third Circle Breath

The extreme Third Circle breath is one where the chest is seen to be puffed and held out as far as it can go. The intake is noisy and it can seem that a Third Circle breather is actually taking our oxygen with their own. There can be a force in the intake that can suck others in. The intake and release can be overcontrolled, not allowing the breath to organically respond to external or internal impulses. It is a forceful and controlling breath showing no vulnerability. If the intake takes energy out of the room then the outward breath can seem to flatten others.

Third Circle breath can have holds in the breath which put huge pressure on the chest, lower back and neck, to the extent that veins can appear in the neck. Breathing is not a joy but an act of effort and control. This breath produces a loud but pushed voice. There is no subtlety in the sounds, no give or take. The voice cannot express appropriately the nuances of thought or feeling but sounds get stuck. The too regular control of the rhythm of the breath can appear uncaring, even robotic. This breath works in limited scenarios. It is found in presentations that are controlling but boring.

Second Circle Present Breath

As you go through the following exercise to use Second Circle breath, a sense of release and emotional connection will increase and I realize it can sometimes be upsetting or create a sense of panic. In my experience, this release, if you have the courage to move through it and breathe it, will not only empower you but unburden your body. As you are on the floor and gravity is placing and relieving you of your tension you will be able to experience the beauty of your natural breath. The breath that will empower you, your presence and voice.

- Begin by returning to the deep release exercise you did for the body. Lie on your back with your calf muscles resting on a chair that allows your thigh muscles to be at right angles to the floor. You might need a small cushion under your head so that your head doesn't pull back and your upper chest doesn't lift.

- Place one hand on your upper chest and one on your stomach.

- Keep the shoulders released and constantly check that your neck, jaw and thighs stay released.

- Use the hand on your chest to remind you that as you breathe in (through your nose), the upper chest doesn't lift. Your hand on the lower abdominal area is a physical reminder that you need to allow movement from the breath down into your lower body.

- For several minutes do nothing but breathe in and out through your nose.

- Try to slow down the rhythm of your breath to its simplest and slowest movement.

- Breathe silently.

- After several minutes take your hands away from monitoring duty and lay them by your sides.

- Keeping the breath slow and silent, take a mental journey through your body to check in on its state. If you encounter tension, remind that tension it can go!

- Start with the jaw into the back of the neck. Visit the shoulders and upper chest. Remind the shoulderblades that they can open and use the floor for support. As you move down the spine, notice how much of the back is being supported by the floor.

- It is quite likely that as the back releases you will feel an ache around the loosening muscles. Feel your buttocks and pelvic area supported by the floor and the stomach muscles released. This release is directly connected to the relaxation of the thighs and will make the groin area feel extremely vulnerable.

- You will come across sections of the body that fail to

open and you might want to stop breathing as you meet those areas. However, try to keep the breath fluid in and out. Although this is uncomfortable, it is also invaluable. The areas that are hard to release and breathe into are the areas that contain your primary tensions.

- Now place your hands around the centre of your body and find your ribcage.

- Feel the sides of the ribcage and feel any movement of breath and then slide your hands back to feel the movement in the back of the ribcage. On the inward breath the ribcage opens around the centre of your torso, without the shoulders or upper chest lifting. After the ribs move out and up, muscles in the stomach, abdominal area and pelvis release and move out. On the outward breath all these muscles – the ribcage and the lower muscles – move in and create a column of air that will support your power and sound and consequently send that energy into the world.

- Now interchange the breath through the nose and mouth. The nose breath is calmer but you will also need the mouth.

- Even in these simple movements you might identify locks or holds that impede your presence. You might feel the need to lock up your ribcage, puff it out and hold it and then force the air out. You might find it hard to breathe into the lower area, not finishing the breath, and then depressing the chest on the exhale.

At this point I want you to pause as you breathe in and out on the floor.

The pause is because I want you to work on one of the most important aspects of your power. In fact, I consider the next piece of work one of the most crucial things I can teach about presence and power.

When your power is being eroded or attacked – for whatever reason – there is a clear indication of this in your breathing. *Everything* that happens to you manifests firstly in your breath. The pattern and rhythm of your breathing is a clear indication of where you are in your power and presence.

As you breathe in, there is a clear moment when the breath is suspended – not locked but present in your body, before you breathe out. This is the moment that places you into the Second Circle. If you act and speak when you are ready then you not only have a chance to be powerful and consequently lead, but will signal to the world your complete power. You fail when you act or speak outside your readiness.

- As you lie there breathing, begin to identify this moment of readiness. If your habit is First Circle you won't dare to wait. You will want to breathe out a fraction of a second before the breath suspends and is fully present in your body. You might even weaken yourself further by deflating as you reach that moment of full power. A Third Circle habit will try to lock the suspension into place or overinflate the breath. This attempt to control the readiness only achieves a block and loss of power.

- Take time to investigate this moment without reduction of force and when you feel this readiness, release on a light 's' sound.

- So breathe in, feel the suspension and readiness of the breath and then breathe out using the ribcage and abdominal muscles to support the 's'.

- After a few releases you should feel the breath is in contact with the 's' sound. This breath contact or connection is what I call support.

- Take time and enjoy the ease and simplicity of this release.

- As soon as you have experienced the readiness and release of breath on the 's', which is a concentration in the intake of breath, concentrate on the release.

- As the breath supports the 's' there is a moment when you know you should take another breath. You can go on with the release of the 's' but it is going on without full power or support. In fact, if you experiment with going on you can feel parts of your body constricting to conserve the breath by closing around it or holding it.

- In the natural breath you take what you need, release what you need, speak when you are ready and breathe when you need. Observe anyone who has real and authentic power and you will see this breath in action.

- Spend a few minutes breathing with that clarity, responding to your body's needs.

- You can extend and feel this release more sensually if you change the sound to a 'z' and then gently pull your knees towards you with your hands. After several releases in this position you should be feeling breath connection and support clearly. Replace your legs on the chair and return to a silent and calm breath.

You have spent a considerable amount of time on the floor and I know that in many lifestyles time is a huge luxury and it is impracticable to be doing this work every day. Many people express a sense of 'I can't take this time for myself'. Other responses include (particularly when I do floor work with people), 'but I don't speak lying on the floor'.

Of course you don't but let us get this in perspective. As you lie on the floor, gravity takes care of many of the tensions you have embedded in your body over the years.

Floor work is a rapid way of addressing them. The time spent on the floor breathing will change you quicker than time spent rushing around seeking something that can only be found by taking time. You need to honour time. Spend time working in order to change and be good at what you do. Deep work takes time, and don't believe anyone who tells you otherwise.

Even a few sessions on the floor will help you understand where work needs to be done and you might only need to revisit these floor exercises when extremely stressed or fraught.

Think about this work as the foundation of all the more strengthening and practical work that follows. You will be able to refer back to the sensations felt on the floor during the next stages of work and when you are actually presenting and using your power.

This work does take time but it has the worth of platinum in all aspects of your life.

You are still on the floor so let's get you up.

- Remove your legs from the chair and roll on to your side.

- Lie there and enjoy the release around your shoulders and neck, and feel the heaviness of your arms.

- Feel the breath around your body.

- Move on to your hands and knees and allow your bottom to collapse on to the calf muscles, your forehead to rest on the floor, and your arms to rest on the floor above your head.

48

- Release your shoulders and neck.

- Some people find this position too painful – if that is the case, come up and centre the body – but if it is bearable you will be able to place a deep breath into your back.

- As you breathe in this position (called the child position in yoga) your back will naturally open and you will feel the abdominal muscles, although restricted by your thighs, actively engage.

- In this position you can clearly sense the readiness of your breath.

- After taking a few breaths here, slowly sit back on your feet, place the spine up, and allow the shoulders to release. You will now feel the breath go down deeply into your lower abdominal power base. Place a hand there and release on a 'z' from this low support.

- You will start to contact your full breath power. It could feel exciting and even too easy!

- Now, get to your feet, coming up carefully. As you stand, check the position of your feet on the floor, with the weight forward and the feet hip-width apart.

- You will feel spaced out but look around you and focus on an object across the room to bring you back into Second Circle.

- Resist placing yourself back into any physical or breath habits. This could be a spinal slump and rounding of the shoulders or holding up your chest.

- It is inevitable that the tensions that have fallen off you will make you feel very open and vulnerable, and you might want to reduce yourself into First Circle or defend yourself into a Third Circle placing.

- Place your concentration on your breathing and hopefully it feels calmer and is moving deeper into the body.

- Invest in the feeling of readiness in the breath and check that it is there for you.

- Walk over to a wall and gently push against it as you did in the body-work section, but this time notice as you push whether the breath is low and connected in your body.

- While pushing against the wall, release on a 'z' and see if you can identify the breath's power.

- When you feel the power, this push can be done with one hand and be very subtle. Later you will be able to reconnect your breath when under pressure in all aspects of your life and regain any lost power with unseen pushes against tables, desks and chairs!

- You can equally feel this connection by holding a chair above your head and breathing and then releasing on 'z'.

- After coming away from the wall or putting the chair down, you can maintain that connection if you don't return to old habits.

- Repeat until you stay connected and after being connected you will be able to switch this connection on at will.

- Now try walking with purpose, keeping the breath free, and when you stop, avoid going backwards in your body or deflating the breath (First Circle), or holding or locking the breath (Third Circle). This practice can be done anywhere. You can walk in the street, then stop and check that your body and breath are connected and are present in you.

What you are precisely working is the full Second Circle engagement of the intake of breath – the connection to you taking your power. Now we have to work on the full release of your power into the world and into specific points of Second Circle focus. That is, your power specifically touching the world outside you.

- Start by imagining you are throwing a ball underarm.

- A good throw is done on the outbreath. By the way, this work will improve any sport you engage in that propels a ball!

- Your arm swings back as you inhale and the arm then suspends with the breath. Release on the outbreath, and as you swing the arm forward the ball is sent. At the moment you need to breathe in, your arm will swing back, taking in the breath energy ready to repeat the process as the arm swings to a place of suspension and readiness with the breath. The ball is thrown on the outbreath – not before or after the breath is ready, and you will swing back to take breath when you need it without any holds.

If you are throwing the ball in First Circle you will probably not fully complete the inward breath, which corresponds to the backward swing of the arm, and will send the ball before the breath and arm have completed their journey. The ball is being sent with incomplete power and then you probably retreat after throwing the ball.

A Third Circle throw will be forced; you pull in the air as the arm goes back, holding the breath and arm before the throw, which will be too forceful so that the arm is stuck into a lock after the ball has gone.

This exercise seems too simple but it is extremely effective in getting your breath connected to your presence. You are, after all, designed to swing. If you can abandon yourself after a few minutes of swinging, the breath coordinates with you and your body.

If you have a ball and a wall to hand, throw the ball against the wall and catch it a few times. The breath begins to work naturally.

One of the reasons juggling makes you so present is that you can only juggle successfully when the breath is working naturally. Any sport involving swings will engage the breath in this way: you will vastly improve your golf swing and tennis stroke with this breath awareness. In fact, if you return to any memory of a fantastic stroke, throw or kick in your favourite sport, you are likely to remember that the breath was effortless and worked with the natural support.

Breathing Energy

The next exercise is crucial in taking your energy into every situation, changing the energy around you and presenting with your full power and presence.

- Stand centred and get the breath as low into the body as possible.

- Look at an object across the room (an empty chair is a good choice).

- Make sure your body stays forward and present to this object.

- Breathe to the object. Touch it with your breath.

- As you breathe in don't pull away. You are breathing to the object and then taking breath from it.

Observe what happens to you and your breath if you only breathe halfway across the room to the object. You will be pulled into First. If you don't breathe to and into a person or room, you are pulling your energy back into yourself and not filling the space. Observe how breathing past your object will push you into Third. You have disconnected by going beyond the point of your concentration with your breath. Crucially, if you breathe beyond us, your audience, we feel bulldozed or irrelevant; you are somewhere else, beyond us!

The point of this exercise is to help you breathe in Second Circle to a room of people in a way that will keep you and them engaged. You will fill the space with your energy and you will take energy from them. This equally applies to smaller meetings, one-to-one conversations, interviews, telephone conversations, even emails and text messaging. Your breath pattern is infectious. When you are present in your breath then your audience has a chance to be present with you. You are actually helping them listen. When you breathe in this way with the content of your presentation, you own what you are saying and share it with others.

Those who don't wish you well try subconsciously to knock the breath out of you by not breathing to you. You then have a choice. With this knowledge you can continue to breathe powerfully and fully in your presence even when those around you are not. In this way you can defeat the workplace bully, stay present in the interview that has been designed to humiliate or frighten you, or stay attentive when the boring CEO is beguiling the rest of you into submission. You have a real chance to stay present when you breathe in this way and no real chance if you don't.

Summary

- The breath enters silently either through the nose or mouth – without lifting the shoulders or upper chest. The ribcage opens all around the centre of your body and a release is felt into the lower abdominal area.

- You feel a readiness or suspension in the breath and you then breathe out.

- Just as you feel that the support muscles have released to their fullest and before you constrict the body in any way, you breathe again with ease.

- You breathe to the space and people in that space.

Practise these principles and your communication and effectiveness will be transformed. You will start to touch your full power.

Breathing For Constant Voice Use

If you need to use your voice in large arenas or for several hours a day, you will need to extend your breath strength, capacity and consistency. Great communication takes work and application and if you can do even a few minutes of the following exercises your vocal fitness will grow.

Keep reminding yourself of all the bodywork and the principles of the breath and support already worked on. You are now beginning to build on your techniques and craft. You are about to get stronger and fitter.

Rib Stretches

The breath needs muscles so let's start with the ribcage.

The muscles around the ribcage go very quickly so if you have a few days off and then have to present in a big space, do these stretches the day before you present and on the morning of the presentation.

- Stand centred in Second Circle and keep checking the body for any useless tensions.

- Keep upright with your knees and ankles soft.

- Allow the left arm to arc over your head so that you flop over to your right.

- Breathe in and out in this position, then stand upright and you will feel a stretch and an opening on the left side of the ribcage.

- Repeat, but this time pull the arched arm with your right hand.

- As you breathe in and out you will feel a bigger stretch and the breath will begin to go lower into the abdominal area.

- As the stretches get bigger you should identify the moment of readiness in the breath and the support that goes with this breath presence.

- Now stretch the right side of your ribcage by repeating this sequence with your right arm.

When both sides are done you will feel calmer and wider and readier for action.

This next exercise is a mighty stretch of the breath, particularly the back of the ribcage. If this works for you it will be one that you rely on forever.

When you naturally want to get your breath back into the body – for instance after running – you automatically put your hands on your bent knees and lean over. In this position the back of the ribcage opens. All I am adding to this natural position is a hug.

- Keeping your shoulders released, wrap your arms around your body so that they are gently but firmly pressing against your chest.

- Bend your knees as far as is comfortable so that you go into a squat.

- When in the squat, take a calm but full breath.

- You will feel the whole of the back open up and a clear sense of engagement and readiness in the breath – don't rush.

- After three or four breaths let your arms flop down, then come up slowly through the spine until you are centred.

- You might feel dizzy, so fix on a point in the room and breathe to it in order to place you and your breath into Second Circle.

- Walk to a wall and push with one hand against it – feel the power of your breath settle in your body.

- Still pushing, take a breath and count 'one'. Feel the support under the 'one', and its energy going into the wall.

- Take a breath and count 'one, two'.

- Build up in this way until you reach the moment when you run out of real support. Don't ever go beyond your support.

- You might be able to reach five or even ten.

- Eventually I would like you to build up to at least 15 on a fully supported breath.

- As soon as you come away from the wall, repeat the exercise with the memory of the push engaging your breath and body. Find a point and count 'one' to it. Find another point and count 'one, two', etc. You are doing an exercise that will eventually help you to effortlessly fill any space with Second Circle energy. If you feel a lack of coordination with the breath as you perform this exercise, add the underarm swing. This will rapidly get you on your breath.

After these exercises you should feel a workout has been done to the ribcage. There is a much smaller version of the hug that opened your back. This can be performed in public without anyone noticing what you are doing but it can save you when you are under pressure and risk losing your power and presence.

- Sit on a chair with your feet fully connected on the floor, and your spine naturally up.

- Lean forward and place your elbows on your knees. Breathe in this position and you will open the back and place the breath low in the body.

I strongly believe that unless you can open the back of your ribcage you have no chance to fully combat fear or stress.

Capacity Exercises

Central to this book is a belief that most of us have not used our voices fully and feel let down by them when communication really matters. One of the most fundamental physical results of vocal underuse is the dramatic reduction of sustainable breath capacity.

We all need breath capacity if we want to speak in larger spaces and with passion. Space and passion require more breath and oxygen and it follows that because we don't express ourselves in this way on a regular basis, the capacity disappears. So in moments of passion or in addressing large numbers of people, many of us find ourselves running out of breath and even gasping.

Some speakers avoid running out of breath by plotting where they take a breath. This can work but is very controlling and not organic and therefore distracting to both speaker and audience. In an ideal world – and I am aiming to place you there, in that world – your breath system should be so good that it works for you in all situations. You shouldn't have to notice or worry about it. With this in mind, I am going to encourage you to invest in three major capacity exercises. They are admittedly repetitive and can seem tedious but will give you so much freedom in all your communication that you will bless the work that you are now going to put in, particularly when you meet unexpected challenges in your presentations.

As you do these exercises, remember the following rules:

- No shoulder tension or lift, particularly on the intake of breath.

- No gasping sound as you breathe in.

- No constriction in the spine, upper chest, shoulders or jaw as you exhale.

- Always work on release with the readiness of breath and take breath when you need it – so you never go beyond your support.

You can do these exercises standing pushing a wall, holding a chair over your head, swinging your arms, walking or sitting, as long as the upper body remains released. If you feel tension that is not shifting, lie on the floor with your legs supported by a chair for the exercises.

- Breathe in calmly and when you feel the suspended readiness of the breath, release over ten seconds on a light 's'. If you can't get to ten seconds go as far as you can with the support. It is not a competition and your capacity will grow and strengthen as you get fitter. Build up to 20 seconds, staying aware of keeping the release steady and sustained. Professional speakers, like stage actors, keep a 30-second capacity as a measure of fitness. With regular exercise, you can double your capacity within a month.

The first exercise increases your capacity but you are only doing one release.

The demands of heightened and passionate speaking will sometimes require a fitness level that has a full capacity release many times in one event. So you have to prepare to get fitter.

- Keep all the principles in place through your body and breath and now release on a 'z' three times in a row. Breathe in, start when you are ready and go as far as you can go without losing support, then breathe in, start again, and repeat. Even after one cycle of these exercises you will feel work has been done and cobwebs are being blown out of your breath system.

- Build up to seven of these breaths one after the other. Be careful that between the breaths you don't pull back into yourself or even walk back. Maintain a point of concentration outside you so that you keep giving out into space.

- Done properly you will feel exhilarated and more alive after the exercise.

- It is often useful at this point to pick up a book or newspaper and read aloud with this free flowing and powerful breath. This demonstrates how free and vibrant the breath can be when properly engaged.

The following exercise might be for later as it is athletic! If you manage to do it without tension creeping up into your shoulders and upper chest you will begin to feel confident that your breath system can work under pressure and survive most demands on it. The essence of the exercise is pace of breath and taking what you need. If, during the exercise, you feel tension, stop as you won't be able to go through this tension and it will only prove counter-productive.

- Stand centred and ready.

- Take enough breath to count 'one'.

- Recover as quickly and as low into the body as you can and count 'one, two'.

- Recover as quickly as you can and count 'one, two, three'.

- In this way, build up to ten.

- When you reach ten, repeat ten, then try even more pace and count over nine.

- Recover and count over eight.

- Recover and count over seven until you are back to one.

- If you managed this without tension, you should feel very present in your breath.

- Repeat and aim to eventually build up to fifteen.

Reading aloud after this will make you feel wonderfully connected and the breath organic to the thoughts and feelings of the reading. With this breath in place you might even understand words and thoughts better. As you breathe more fully and naturally you think and feel in a clearer and more vivid way.

Summary

- Breathing is the mechanism that releases your power into the world, transferring energy outwards.

- Keep your breath regular and balanced, intake and outbreath mirroring each other in intensity, length and depth.

- Focus on your breathing by using the sensations learned through floorwork, and increase the capacity and power of your breath through athletic and dynamic exercise.

VOICE

You were born with a wonderful, free, expressive and power-ful voice. If you need a reminder of that, just listen to the cry of a baby. All that power, range and vigour powered from a tiny body and ribcage and minute vocal folds!

If your voice fails you, in any way, then it is because the body and breath tensions have constricted and blocked your voice. Your voice can fail you in many ways, all of which affect your presence and power. Any vocal failure fills you with fear as your voice expresses all of you and if it doesn't work, you don't work. If your voice hurts or tires easily, if your voice is too small or too loud, if your voice does not sound appropriate to what you are saying, if your voice annoys listeners or is easily ignored, you are not present in your voice.

With the body and breath work we have already done, your voice will have improved, but to really extend your effective-ness in communicating you have to understand what your voice does to listeners and how the sound of your voice creates an immediate judgement – a turn-off or a turn-on. The sound of your voice, when it is not free, is not a true reflection of who you are but others will believe it is the real you. Your impaired voice communicates an impaired person to the world. Your voice is the tip of an iceberg. Underneath the voice is the whole of your being and it is distressing if your voice doesn't serve the wholeness of you. It is never too late to find your whole free voice.

So many people say to me, 'I am much more interesting than I sound,' or 'my voice lets me down.' I have to say that on a weekly if not daily basis I meet brilliant, powerful, gentle and delightful people who have been ignored, misconstrued or resented because of the sound of their voice. To put it simply, they have not been known or fully explored by others because of a small tension in their voice. They have been judged and abandoned because their voice is not easy to listen to. So it is essential that you learn about your voice and sound and that means you must work to free and place your voice.

Let us start with your own knowledge of your voice. What are the reactions to your voice? If you have the physical and breath habits of First Circle, you will have one or maybe all of the following reactions:

- You are often hard to hear.

- You are often asked to repeat yourself.

- Your voice lulls people into drowsiness and you can even see their eyes glaze over when you speak for any length of time.

- People lean forward to hear you.

- Your voice could be described as sweet or nice or 'girlish' but with that vocal quality you are not expected to say anything important.

- Your voice may sound hazy or like a whisper.

- Under pressure your voice might weaken even more, go higher or squeaky, knot up in your throat and even cut out.

Your reactions to your voice when it doesn't work for you will include anger that you are being ignored and that anger might force your general First Circle nature into an aggressive and harsh Third Circle which will turn more people off! I am afraid that the brutal truth is that if you have a First Circle voice, then you are reliant on the sensitivity and kindness of others to be attentive towards you. So if you are addressing less sensitive people who don't have to listen, they will actively switch off. From their point of view, they are getting no help from you so why should they bother to be attentive?

In short, if you are First Circle and use your voice in First Circle you will never be able to compete in high-powered and pressurized arenas. You might have been successful in your career so far using First Circle in one-to-one gentle encounters as a sensitive listener and sounding board. Your voice might only have become a real issue when you were promoted and required to address groups with clarity and passion, showing your full power and leadership qualities. The only leaders I have encountered who can manage to lead with a First Circle voice are those who have been born to lead and have never had to work at being dynamic or generous in their communication style. They have assumed, in a very deep part of themselves, that they have a right to be a leader and do not have to work in any way themselves to justify that position. These assumptions do not satisfy the people they lead as most of those under the 'I am born to lead' leaders are enraged at the assumption but feel impotent to tackle the carelessness. Interestingly, the 'born-to-lead' communicator can only survive in good times; when a crisis hits they have to become actively present or they are deposed. At this moment in time, I am receiving many cries for help from those who have always assumed that their power was a given and they didn't need to work to communicate. Not any more. Even if you are brilliant at what you do, the time demands that you lead with vocal clarity and humanity, i.e. Second Circle presence.

Many women are very successful in their careers being a caring First Circle manager and then face all the problems of First Circle voice when they are promoted to more powerful positions. I have begun to notice sensitive men suffering in the same way. They have learnt to be caring and in First

Circle and, with a promotion, struggle to find their full presence and power.

Reactions to the Third Circle voice will include one or all of the following:

- Your voice pushes people back, it is too intrusive, penetrating and loud and if you have any sensitivity, you might have seen people wince as you present.

- Children with sensitive ears have been seen to cover them when you present.

- The audience leans back into First Circle.

- Your voice defies interruption so that the audience feels a sense of resignation because they can't get in and affect you, or you find that people suddenly get very aggressive towards you. In other words, you will bring out the habitual First or Third Circle in your audience as they can't be present to you.

- It is possible that people might enjoy your energy, as it can be enthusiastic or joky, but they don't hear content; they only experience your general energy.

- Your voice might be commented on and even commended but your words and ideas lost.

- Your voice could be beautiful but in Third Circle beauty without meaning is useless in a powerful presentation and is not authentic.

- Your belief in your ability to pump out vocal energy is married to a belief that audiences have to be controlled and harnessed.

- You speak at them, not to them.

- Your vocal style might have served you well but somewhere you know you are an interrupter and not a very good listener.

- As you present you believe you have all the answers.

- At some point, probably in one-to-one situations, you have met negative criticism about your lack of vocal sensitivity.

Your generalized vocal energy isn't working anymore. It never did but because you were speaking to perceived inferiors, no-one dared tell you. Higher status colleagues probably find you and your voice tiresome and this has started to erode your confidence. I do believe the work of abandoning these habits of force is very hard for habitual Third Circle communicators because it requires a humility and sensitivity most Third Circle speakers have never had time or reason to require. Most Third Circle speakers come to me because they can't move up until they are better team leaders; people they work with don't trust them. They have had comments about their insensitivity to others and anger issues. Many have had to face the harsh fact that they are perceived as bullies. Then many have come because Third Circle has made them lonely. I promise you that as you abandon this cosmetic power, you will have more success, be better and more human leaders and you won't be lonely and will be able to ask for help.

Freeing Your Voice

The first stage of placing your voice out into the world is freeing your voice of any tensions. You are now working on the next stage of your presence and power and as you do this voice work it is *essential* that you continually check the previous stages of your practice, keeping your body and breath in Second Circle. It is always easy when working on isolated areas of your being to forget connection to the whole of you. The voice is housed in the body and powered by breath. Constantly remind yourself of these elements as you work.

Firstly you must begin to understand where and how you hold your voice. Not only is this essential when you work to free your voice but the knowledge will give you a chance to monitor and correct your presentation, particularly when under pressure in important moments of communication.

First Circle Voice

The energy of your voice is imploding, being pulled back into your throat, mouth or chest. You voice rarely touches your lips, let alone the world, so articulation and clear speech are almost impossible to achieve.

The withdrawal of vocal energy will be felt in the mouth, the jaw is likely to be tight, the throat will feel blocked so that the saying 'a lump in my throat' is an accurate description of the blockage you feel and is intensely felt when a First Circle voice tries to express a passionate emotion. Your words feel swallowed and after extended use, the voice will feel tired or even husky.

Third Circle Voice

If you are forcing or pushing out sound, you will experience a friction in the throat. If you do this a lot you might have a sore throat or even lose all or some of your voice after presentations or stressful meetings. Although you can make loud sounds, the voice will feel and sound immovable. By that, I mean that the range and volume get stuck so that there is no variety in the voice or ability to moderate volume. The voice stays in one place and refuses to move from that place. The voice might reach the front of your mouth and you might speak clearly but the clarity is overcontrolled, with articulation feeling and sounding ponderous. Your instinct as you present is to overwork and this effort can be felt throughout the body: chest overbraced, breath overbreathed and held, neck and jaw pushed forward and even the back of your tongue held.

When you free and place your voice, one of the biggest struggles is 'I am not loud enough or doing enough, it can't be this easy.' It can be easy as long as the work is in the right place, which is the breath support and placing of the voice. What voice work is aiming to achieve is an effortless release powered by breath with the work being efficient and in the right place. Here's an image. Watch a swan swim across a lake. The body above the water is relaxed and serene, but under the water the webbed feet are working hard but efficiently.

The Work

- Sit with your spine in Second Circle, shoulders released and upper chest open.

- Your feet should be on the floor with a concentration of energy forward on the balls of your feet. Breathe low and calmly, identifying the moments when the breath is suspended and ready. Stay in this position and move yourself through a few imaginative processes.

- Without actually speaking, imagine that you are about to speak and see what reactions are triggered in your throat, jaw, face or tongue. This small and subtle check might give you clear notice of your tensions, as the expectancy of speech is often enough to reveal key tensions. Try to recognize even the slightest blockages or tics of tension. These small flickers of muscle tension will be of enormous use to you as this work continues. Is there a slight withdrawal through your body or a slight pushing forward? Is there any hint of closure in your throat, clenching or thrusting forward of the jaw, tightening of face muscles or bunching up of the tongue?

- Now add more pressure to that expectancy and imagine having to speak to the person you most fear speaking to. This will expose your tensions more vividly. You will feel tension in the body and breath but breathe through that tension to discover the vocal tension on top of the breath. You will likely either experience a First Circle swallowing and withdrawing or a Third Circle closing and constriction that you are prepared to push through – the equivalent of a vocal call to arms as a shield to any intrusion or attack.

- Now imagine the best listener you have ever had in your life present in the room and examine whether any tensions fall away from you with this sense of peace, the knowledge of being heard and accepted. If you manage to discover an ease, stay with it and remembering to breathe, perform the next series of exercises. If you find no ease in the last exercise, still work the voice muscles, staying connected to the breath.

- Gently massage your face and jaw hinges. Take time and pay particular attention to the jaw and the point between your eyes. After the massage, check if your face feels different.

- Gently massage the back of your neck and then extremely gently your whole neck. Feel the larynx and massage around it very carefully. Massage up under your chin and begin to release the back of your tongue through the underbelly of your chin. After these simple massages, check how the face and neck feel.

- At this stage, look into a mirror and see if you look different.

- Re-place any tensions in the face, jaw or tongue that you know are part of any of your blocked energies. You might observe how your tensions put a mask on to your face in order for you to face the world.

- Particularly look for these tensions between the eyes and into the forehead.

- Look around the jaw, observe any clenching of the teeth, pulling back of cheek muscles or even needing to smile too much!

- Are the lips too tight, bunched or loose?

- Look at the neck and see if it is taut or flickering with tension.

- Using a mirror as a constant check, move through the next series of exercises.

- Bunch up all the facial muscles and then allow them to release without re-placing the habits. As soon as you feel the need to re-place any tension you have gone back to your habits. Even if you can't feel these tensions you will see your habit in action in the mirror. Do this at least three times.

- Push your lips forward and then pull them back into a grimace. Repeat three times. Allow the lips to find their own placing, don't re-place the habits. Feel and watch these exercises.

- Open your mouth as wide as possible, followed by a release. Repeat three times. Where does your mouth want to be?

- Stretch your tongue by placing it outside your mouth, trying to keep it parallel to the floor. Repeat three times.

After this sequence of exercises, come back to rest and feel any change in the placing of muscles. Your lips should be together but the teeth not clenched. The face should not be placed, and therefore, as you look at yourself, it is neutral. The face is open, but not conveying any emotion or attitude. Your facial mask is beginning to drop.

This next exercise begins to open out any tension in your throat and is one that will be effective under pressure when you feel yourself closing down or wanting to push through tension.

- Check your body and breath are in Second Circle.

- Return to the neutral face.

- Slowly begin to smile until you feel your cheek muscles spread into a wide smile but with your lips together. You will feel the smile in your ears.

- Gradually, but keeping the wide smile in place, open your mouth as far as you can without any force. A guideline is that the space should always accommodate the width of two fingers in your mouth. However, if this stretch is too much, release the jaw to the widest opening possible without pressure.

- Release the jaw and return to the neutral face without any clenching in the jaw or back of the throat.

- At this stage, most people can identify small grips of tension that want to reintroduce themselves in the jaw or throat. It is essential they don't reappear so do the exercise until you can control any reappearance of any jaw or throat tension.

Repeat this exercise adding a very crucial breath quality which will be a clear reference to keeping your vocal instrument open.

- Smile and open the mouth and at the mouth's widest position, breathe in and out SILENTLY and SLOWLY. No noise and no rush. There should not be a hint of a rasp, a 'ha' or a gasp because if you hear any sounds on the inhalations or exhalations, there is a closure of some sort in the passage of air and this closure will translate into a closure in the voice as you use it, particularly under pressure and when you need to draw on your full power.

- If you can hear a sound, rerelease your shoulders, neck and upper chest and help the throat open by imagining a yawn. This will open you and when you can allow the flow of air through your body silently, you will feel an open channel of supported air from your lower abdomen to the outside world. You are open and allowing air, which is energy, into your body and then out of your body into the world, freely, without blocking. You are connected to yourself through air and to the world through your air freely going out.

- When you return to neutral, count aloud to ten with that open channel and your voice will have already begun to feel freer.

- First Circle voices will feel a new richness to their sound. Third Circle voices will experience a new ease.

Repeat this exercise and now add in a release of the tongue.

- Smile, open the jaw, breathe in and out silently and then stretch the tongue, fully over the chin but without hurting the tongue.

- When you have stretched it, release it and without your help it will slide into your mouth and find its position at the bottom of the mouth with the back released and less bunched up. Repeat three times.

- The back of the tongue is huge and without this stretch it can block off your voice and constrict or hold it back. First Circle speakers allow the tongue to pull their speech energy back and Third Circle speakers push through this blockage.

- Now count aloud again and you should feel the voice has opened up even more. It is richer and more effortless.

During these exercises, you will probably have experienced a yawn sensation and maybe have used the imagined yawn as a way of opening the voice. We use the yawn as it is a natural way for the body to open the throat and receive more oxygen. This is why you yawn when trying to stay awake or even when confronting huge emotions. The body is reacting with a yawn to get the throat open and receive more oxygen to cope.

You can use the yawn as a reliable technique to open your throat and free the voice. In fact, decades ago, actors were trained to speak on the edge of a yawn so that they could maintain a released voice. The downside of that technique is that those actors sounded too open and often pompous. Obviously, I don't want you to sound like that but imagining a yawn can dig and release tension out of your voice. It is a technique that has saved many voices because it is an immediate release that can stop profound tension damaging the vocal folds. A high-powered bully who was working with me to stop his intimidating ways reported that the yawn technique was useful to him when he found he wanted to attack. He recognized that the first signs of attack started in the tightening of his jaw and closing of his throat. The thought of a yawn released these tensions and stopped him from pouncing inappropriately.

So try this and remember to breathe fully and silently while you do this exercise.

- Think of yawning and on the edge of the yawn, move into speaking. In effect, you are speaking on the edge of a yawn.

- Try counting with this imagined yawn. Your voice will sound odd but the vocal instrument in your throat will be freer.

- Then count without the yawn and your voice will be much freer.

Eventually, the yawn technique will be so subtle that you can release the throat when it is closing down on you by a single thought of yawning. You can use this technique as tension builds up in your throat before speaking or when an emotion is beginning to destroy your ability to stay in control of a situation.

You can even use the thought of yawning to stop those threatening and choking coughs that visit you in theatres or concerts!

With all these exercises done, your vocal instrument is more open but you have to extend your voice more to get it into Second Circle presence. So many presenters fail because they haven't warmed up their voices. We all know we cannot do any extended physical activity without a good physical warm-up. The same principle applies to the voice. Without a warm-up the voice will let you down.

This hum is a basic voice warm-up and you will learn to warm up your voice with humming before any demanding presentation.

- On and with the breath, begin to gently hum.

- Keep breathing and anytime you feel the voice tighten as you hum, check all the areas of tension until you can maintain a gentle but sustained hum without tension. Hum until you feel that the voice motors smoothly and can be sustained.

The voice is rather like those old cars with chokes: until the car was warmed up it spluttered and stumbled along. Hum until it voices without hesitation. The voice warms up during the day so early morning events take more warming up. Some days it will take a few minutes, other days it might take up to ten minutes. The voice also needs hydration so it will work better if you drink lots of room temperature water (ice cold won't help when 'warming up').

At any point if you feel the voice close, stop and check on the body, breath and vocal tensions, release them and continue.

- When the voice feels warmed by the humming, stand up and walk with energy until you really feel in your Second Circle body.

- Pick up a reading and stand side on to a wall.

- Place one hand against the wall and push gently until you feel your breath engage.

- Read aloud with this push in place, all the time monitoring your tensions and, if necessary, stopping to release them.

- After reading out a 90-second section, come away from the wall and read the same section.

- The voice will be freer but First Circle speakers might feel that it is too free and loud and Third Circle speakers the reverse – that it is not enough and too easy.

- This is a moment you have to trust. If your voice feels freer and you are breathing then it is better. At this stage you must stop controlling and judging so that you can move forward into your presence.

At this stage you have put into place the three foundation stones of all voice and presentation work – body, breath and voice. You might like to pause here and stay connected to all you have achieved with refinding your natural body, breath, voice and self. You might wish to dwell on this work, practise and excel with the stages you have achieved and work it until it feels organic before moving into the next stages of presence.

Here are two observations I've made over many years. If you tend towards First Circle you might be fearful of moving into the next stage and stay too long on this work as a way of avoiding Second Circle voice. A Third Circle person is always tempted to move ahead before they have learnt any work deeply; they are impatient. So you might want to hesitate or push on too quickly. Be aware and use your judgement to either move on or stay with the previous work for deep organic connection.

Placing the Voice in Second Circle

There is no doubt in my mind that placing a free sound out into a space, towards an audience and on to a specific focus, can be terrifying. If you're used to First Circle and its imploding sound and words, you are not risking anything as you speak – your words are not out there, so what you say doesn't matter! If your voice leaves you in Third Circle through filters of pushed tension, then people hear your words through a distortion of sound and this distraction actually shields you from their reaction. No-one really knows through your words your authenticity, your heart, what you actually think, or your vulnerability. In this way, speaking has no risk. You do not have to stand by what you say!

It is good to remind ourselves what the ancient Greeks believed. When you place your words out into the world freely and to specific targets then your words create what you are saying as you say it. At the moment of speech, your truth exists, your words live.

This way of speaking is extremely difficult to do in a world that doesn't want truth, passion or gravitas. But it is the only way to communicate if you want to transform anyone, or any situation. I believe the world can be saved with Second Circle words. There is the hope but if we do not stay present with ourselves and our words there is no hope of any level of transformation and action. In effect, we have all become powerless and only deal with cosmetic and unimportant power.

No-one wants a leader, an elder or a parent that cannot, when required, speak with true power, clarity and authenticity.

Let Us Try To Put Ourselves Clearly And Authentically Out Into The World

Your voice releases from you on an arc. It moves up and out and when it has presence, touches a target across space. You know this if ever you have had to call across space. Imagine throwing a dart: you arc it and then it lands on the board. This throw is how you place your voice.

'Throwing' Your Voice

- Stand and find a point across the room just above the eyeline.

- As you fix yourself on that point, come slightly forward through your body to that point. Enter that point through your body's imagination. You will feel this through your feet up to your head. Stay alert to the point or target.

- Now breathe to that point. At the end of each breath, stay connected freely to the point. Don't pull or slump off the target (First) or brace your body and force the connection (Third).

- Hum freely to the point until you feel a buzz on your lips. This will also mean the jaw must be free. When you feel the buzz sustained on your lips this is an indication that the voice is ready to leave you and enter the world.

- Go to a wall and repeat the reading exercise with your hand pushing against the wall.

- This will take at least 90 seconds of reading to exercise this placing. After reading, come away from the wall and read to the point or target.

- Your voice should be more placed and connected. And you will feel words clearer in your mouth.

During the reading, First Circle speakers might sense their words dropping off from the target so try to maintain connection. Third Circle speakers might have to fight an urge to push to get connected to the target.

This next exercise is more revealing. It places the voice further forward and out than most people have done since they freely cried out from their cradle!

- Engage the whole body and breathe to a point just above the eyeline.

- Breathe in and on the breath, release on an 'ooh'. Deliberately move your lips forwards, not in a tight pursing but in a forward funnel, so you can feel the energy buzzing forward on your lips.

- Imagine and then feel the sound moving towards the point on your breath up through your throat, arching into the head and into the small 'o' made by your lips, and out.

- Voice a comfortable note. You are successful even if you feel that you hit the point with your voice for a few seconds. Your voice is now in Second Circle and present to and in the world.

- Repeat this 'ooh' several times. This is an exercise you will perform whenever you need to place your voice.

- After several releases, begin to monitor your energy more precisely. Is the 'ooh' hitting the target but then falling off? You will be able to feel this clearly with the 'ooh', even if you can't yet feel it in speech. The equivalent in speech is the doomed falling line when sentences fall down a plughole. It is impossible to listen to, a vocal kiss of death, boring or lulling the audience into a pessimistic despair!

- Imagine finishing the sound or word outside you, not pulled back into you (First). Also be careful not to push or force the energy, which will pull you up into Third.

- At this moment the pushing exercise you have done has a new and dynamic use. Go to a wall and gently push, engage the breath and then release on the 'ooh'. The contact through the wall with your hand will be a wonderful guide to whether the sound is falling or being wrongly forced. Sound is physical and you will feel its energy through your hand. A First Circle speaker will feel the hand pull away from the wall. Third Circle speakers will be pushing too hard and tightening around the upper chest, neck and jaw. Many speakers swear by this push and 'ooh' to prepare their vocal presence.

It is about to get harder but also more revealing and more useful to your understanding of your voice and presence. You are now ready to build on all the exercises you've done. The body, breath, free voice and placing.

This exercise will not only prepare you for any vocal challenge, but help you to discover all the deep vocal habits that constrict you. Doing this exercise will give you a superb foundation of vocal release into Second Circle which will change your ability to communicate directly in all circumstances.

- Repeat everything that you have done up to this point. That is, place an 'ooh' to your point above the eyeline.

- Now go from the 'ooh' into an open 'ah', keeping the sound open and free. This is easier said than done.

As you enter the sound 'ah' from an 'ooh' you might want to withdraw it back into your mouth and throat or overcontrol and force it with tension. 'Ah' makes us all feel emotionally vulnerable and the responses you chart in your voice are clear and uncompromising. You might need to spend weeks experimenting on 'ooh' into 'ah', keeping it open, forward and sustained to a target.

- You might well need to use the thought of a yawn to keep the sound free.

- Send 'ooh' into 'ah' around the room to different points.

- Use the wall push or the throwing action as a physical energy release.

- Release for a count of three on 'ooh' moving into an 'ah' for a count of seven. When you can achieve this, try different notes and different levels of volume.

These basic exercises will build up muscular strength capacity and consistency in the whole of your vocal apparatus.

The next exercise marries every technical process you have worked on up to now. It is the exercise of intoning, which is releasing on full breath, with an open and placed voice on one note. This fluid release is like a one-note chant. It is a full and flowing movement of your voice. The human voice is designed to intone and sing and it is therefore the most natural and freeing vocal position you can adopt. Many people are so frightened of singing, which is akin to intoning, that they forget to use their voice in its most powerful form.

- Engage all of yourself to a point above the eyeline.

- Start by sending a rapid series of 'mah mah mah mahs' to this point.

- Now move from 'mahs' to 'moos'.

- Using a comfortable single note, release an intoned series of words to that point. It could be counting or a line of reading. Here's one.

'Roll on there deep dark ocean roll.'

Byron

Breathe and intone several times. Repeat until the voice and breath feel free and are flowing.

Intone over numbers or a line and then take a breath and speak the words to the point. Repeat this process. Intone and then speak.

Now intone the line and move into speaking on the same breath.

Even after a few minutes of this process your voice will begin to flow out of you with its natural power and freedom.

Intone a whole section of a reading that lasts at least two minutes – remember to breathe when necessary and keep the throat open, maybe with the thought of a yawn.

When you have finished the reading and before you have time to think or contemplate the exercise, speak the reading.

The voice will have more body and freedom and will also reach out to the world.

- As you intone you will have to battle your habits – the demons of withdrawal (First) or pushing (Third) – and this battle will continue as you speak. Intoning will prepare your voice for every vocal contact you will ever make and this exercise will be essential to you for years.

- Even within a few weeks of repeating this work you will feel a strengthening and an enriching of your voice.

Maybe you would like to pause here before extending your voice. What you have worked on so far will indeed improve your voice but when you are ready to go on, you can work on your resonance and range.

Resonance and Range

To go even further and have a magnificently effective voice you need to open up its full potential. This potential lies in the full use of your voice through its resonance and range.

Your voice has so much lost potential and I describe most voices I hear as rusty, dusty and full of cobwebs. These cobwebs have to be blown away for you and the world to hear your full vocal potential. When your voice is free and connected to you, your body, breath and the word in Second Circle, it will move freely and organically with thought and feeling. Your voice will become a clear reflection of your authenticity and passion, and sound appropriate to what is being said. Your voice, then, matches what is being thought, felt and said.

Some people who speak in Third are thought to have 'beautiful' voices, but this is really manipulation rather than authenticity, and I'm sure you can tell whether the voice truly matches the person's real thoughts and emotions, their passion and spirit, or is a mask. We have all been in the presence of beautiful speakers but, after the presentation, not known what it was all about.

The next section of exercises is designed to stretch reduced voices and allow your passion to come through your voice with presence.

Resonators

The resonators of the human voice amplify it so that when you use all your resonators, the voice is not only richer and more textured, but easier to release in space. A thin voice is not fully resonated, the whole body of the voice is not being used and therefore vocalization takes more effort. A tight voice limits the resonators.

Your voice resonates throughout your body and there are five main resonators or cavities like a guitar box that give your voice energy, volume and different textures and qualities. Let us examine your resonators and what they add to your voice.

The Chest Resonator This gives your voice its base quality or texture. The chest resonator suggests authority and power. However, if it is used too much, it doesn't help the voice to be projected in space and if it dominates the voice the listener only hears muffled mumblings of sound, and speech is rendered indistinct. When the voice is placed in Second Circle the chest resonator provides a strong vocal foundation and texture without dominating the voice and creating the over-used chest rumble.

You can hear First Circle speakers hide their voice so much that it falls back into their chest and then produces an incoherent creak of sound that is trapped in the lower neck and upper chest. Many people experience that sound when they are exhausted and lack energy to get the voice out. Overuse of chest resonance is common in Third Circle speakers. The voice is forced down into the chest. This creates a bluffed power with the sound bulldozing the listener into submission. When you next experience this quality of voice, note how you hear this quality but cannot fully distinguish the words that are being spoken. The chest quality can be heard as authoritative, threatening or sexy, but it's very limiting when used out of balance.

You do need chest resonance, but in balance to the rest of your voice, and in order to have this resonance with a forward sound, you need strong breath support. The chest sound is very fashionable, so much so that I have encountered people who have been told that their voice lacks power and is too high who have pushed or forced their voice down into the chest. Not only is this counter-productive in the clarity of communication but it can actually tire and even damage the voice. Practically, it is very hard to get any chest resonance if you are carrying shoulder or chest tensions.

The throat resonator is always present in your voice. There is only a problem with the throat resonator if the voice is so de-energized that it stays in the throat and never moves up into the head or mouth. This results in the voice's power being non-existent and clear speech becomes impossible. Third Circle speakers force their voices down into their chest, locking their neck and throat resonator. This habit has the tell-tale signs of veins popping out from the neck. The poor throat resonator becomes squeezed and its vocal quality becomes one of being strangled.

I once worked with a manager who was so blocked in his throat, and his voice was so constricted that he was given the nickname of 'duck'. His voice sounded like a quack and no-one took him seriously until that throat tension was released.

The head, nose and face resonators make up the upper resonators of the voice. When the voice is supported by breath and moves freely up into the mouth to leave you with a Second Circle point of focus, then it will naturally pick up all the three head resonators. These three resonators provide clarity and give your voice the vocal textures that carry in space. It is the energy and power of the head resonators that penetrate space, not the rumble of the chest.

As soon as you allow your voice to be freely amplified in all five resonators, it becomes a balanced and moving sound which enables you to speak with maximum power and efficiency. When the voice is free and fully supported, it will move into the head as you experience any intellectual and emotional excitement.

At some point, listen to a present and powerful speaker who owns their right to speak. You will notice that their voice moves *with* their communication not *against* it – it is a free movement through the resonators. A First Circle speaker can hold back their voice in such a way that power is pushed right up to the top of the head and gets stuck there, becoming shrill and whining. A Third Circle speaker can sound too loud, the voice pushed and sometimes aggressive and intrusive. The voice in Third Circle can bulldoze you. We all know those qualities of sound are very hard to bear and we switch off to defend our ears from them.

Awakening the Head, Nose and Face Resonators

- Sit or stand with a centred Second Circle body.

- Keep breathing with a low breath and a continual connection.

- Monitor your shoulders, upper chest and jaw to keep tension out of these areas and breathe when necessary.

- Place a hand on the top of your head, letting part of the hand touch your forehead.

- Hum into your head.

- Think of the sound going into your head and it will. You might start by only feeling a small buzz but that small buzz is enough to awaken the head resonator.

- Now concentrate on placing sound into your nose.

- Hum into your nose and feel the buzz not only in your nose but under your eyes.

- Now hum into the face, on to the lips and into your cheeks so you are moving sound around your three head resonators.

- The whole quality of your voice will have changed.

Don't worry if it takes time to feel the buzz in each resonator. Eventually your resonators will respond more rapidly as they awaken and respond to sound being placed there. What this series of placed hums will tell you is where you habitually resonate or don't. The underused resonators will need more work but as they come alive they will add power and texture to your voice. Play with placing your hums into all three resonators – head, nose and face – and then pick up a reading and hear how your voice has changed.

Awakening the Throat and Chest Resonators

As you awaken these two resonators, you must be careful not to push down on the voice, so constantly think 'up' to avoid that trap. It is also tempting to tuck your head in and slump the spine as you work these resonances. Humming into the throat is easy but don't allow the throat to close; you might have to remember the yawn and keep everything open.

Moving the voice and humming into the chest is more problematic. You will find it is quite easy to place the voice into the chest and feel dramatic vibrations there but you must avoid pushing down to get this sound. Constantly place this resonator out to a point above eyeline. You will also need more breath and support to resonate in these lower areas of your voice. This extra support will help get your voice into Second Circle.

After awakening your five resonators during these workouts,

your voice will be richer and more varied when you read aloud. The next exercise will show you how to move freely between all five resonators to give you vocal flexibility and the ability to place all the power and amplification of your voice outside you in Second Circle.

Total Resonation

- Place your whole concentration on to a point above the eyeline. Breathe to the point and breathe throughout the exercise when necessary.

- Hum into your head, nose and face and then move down into your throat and chest resonators without dropping the sound back into your throat or chest.

- Move through all five resonators as quickly as you can but keeping contact with the Second Circle point.

- Now speak into each resonator. Some of them will feel alien and the ones that do are the ones that need the most work.

- After stretching your voice out in this way, rest for a few minutes before you get up and go to a wall. Push with one hand to place the breath and speak or read to a Second Circle point outside you.

- You will now be experiencing a much fuller and more textured voice.

Range

The range of your voice is crucial if your voice and presentations are to command interest and engage others. The movement of notes in your voice expresses your range, your true intentions, ideas and feelings. Without range you are not only a dull and lacklustre speaker without the ability to inspire but you are also unable to express your own human complexity. Like all the areas you are working, your range is part of your body, breath and free voice but its movement is very reliant on the state of your resonators so by now, with your resonators cleared of dust and rust, your range has already started to improve.

Discovering More of Your Range

- Find a point above the eyeline.

- Throughout the exercise, keep thinking to this point.

- Keep your head still during the exercise as it will be most tempting to move your head to achieve range, which only results in your head moving the neck muscles rather than the muscles that move your vocal range getting a workout.

- Hum down through your range, thinking up to the point. Do this at least seven times. The voice will start to move more easily after a few swoops down.

- If you find any breaks, gaps or blips in your voice, recognize those insecure areas of your range as they will need extra attention in your range workout. These are probably left over from your youth, as human vocal folds grow at puberty. Boys' voices break as the folds grow. Girls' vocal folds grow but not so dramatically.

For most boys and some girls this breaking or jumping of the voice is a source of acute humiliation and consequently the voice at puberty is controlled and used away from breaks in the range. This avoidance can develop into a very restricted adult range with the voice only being used in 'safe' places.

If you discover any of these break or jumps, however small, you must smooth them away if your voice is to come into its full potential. I do not want you to worry that the voice could break with stress or fear. When you develop your full range you are aiming to stretch out the voice and have your natural limits extended beyond and through limiting breaks wherever they appear. The full extended voice is so exciting to listen to and is part of you.

- Hum down through the voice again and identify the top break, the bottom break and any break or insecure notes in between.

- Recognize the need for good breath support as you stretch your range.

- If there is a break in the main range of your voice, pitch above it and hum down through it.

- Do this several times, thinking up and out to your point.

- Do not attempt to push the voice through the break but flow, with breath, down through it.

- Repeat this enough and breaks begin to smooth out and ultimately go from the main body of your range.

A well-trained voice can move through three octaves of notes and an exciting speaker should aim for at least two octaves of break-free range.

- Now hum down and then move up through the range at least three times.

- Going up through the range might be harder but your vocal flexibility will increase as you repeat these movements.

- Repeat using and placing the sound 'oh' very forward in your mouth, still going up and down.

- Shift the sound into a 'ha' up and down.

- Then speak moving your voice in the same way.

- Count over 20 or read moving up and down through your range as a playful game.

Now your voice has been stretched, you might even feel the stretch in the muscles of your throat; these muscles shouldn't hurt but they should feel worked out. If they do hurt, you have been forcing the stretch in Third Circle and you must do the exercise with ease, breath and not a hint of force. If you feel a stretch in your voice but can't feel any vocal vibrations in your mouth or on your lips then you have done the exercise in First Circle. In both cases, go back and check through your body and breath, and be sure that you are breathing to your point, supporting and vocalizing with the readiness of the breath. Check that the voice is free and the head still when vocalizing through the range.

- After stretching, wait for a few minutes and then read aloud. Concentrate on making sense of the reading and speaking in Second Circle and not consciously thinking about your range – you will naturally be using it now.

Experiencing this sense of freedom in your voice may even create a sense of freedom in your thinking and feeling. The stretching of your range can actually free the internal workings of your mind and heart.

I have had many clients who report that warming up their range before an important meeting or negotiation actually helps them think more clearly.

Summary

- Stay connected to your body and breath as you work to free the voice of tension.

- Practising the yawning technique will open your throat and allow you to stay in control of your voice in stressful situations.

- Using exercises to deepen your intonation and extend your vocal range, the voice will become free and unforced, connecting you with your audience.

SPEECH

Up to now, the muscles you have worked and are beginning to understand are the muscles of your voice, which is the sound of your emotions. Your speech introduces specificity into your voice and reason into emotional sound. The speech muscles clarify the sound of your voice into words, thus carving reason into the emotion of your voice.

The movement of your speech muscles during articulation is an amazing and complex dance going on between your lips, face, tongue, teeth and soft palette.

Clear speech is athletic and those muscles, in order to perform so magnificently, need constant work and fitness tests. Even if you don't speak for a day, your speech muscles will become more sloppy.

First Circle Speech

First Circle speakers fall into the category of mumblers. The voice falling back means that the speech muscles do not have a chance to perform clearly and accurately as there is no vocal energy in the mouth for the muscles to mould. Consequently, ends of words are non-existent and multi-syllabic words are skidded over, blurred and ill-defined. Even when First Circle speakers attempt to speak clearly, their lack of a placed voice can only create the impression of someone overworking speech muscles with very little impact on the clarity of their words. There is a lot of work in the face but with no real results in diction. Sometimes this effort might clarify the beginning of a thought but the second part will disappear with the falling line.

Third Circle Speech

Many Third Circle speakers can overarticulate words by over-stressing them or dwelling on them in such a way that their sense is lost – the words are manipulated and controlled. A Third Circle voice can be so loud, pushed and forced that the articulation is frantic and not only is saliva sprayed out but the words, although articulated, are shot out without aim or target. This can only be confusing to the audience as the words are machine-gunned out without any focus.

Second Circle Speech

Good Second Circle speech is clear, efficient, and seems effort-less. The listener hears the words but does not notice how they are formed or worry that they are not being formed! The word in the mouth is made and forged and then delivered. The voice flows on the breath through the mouth, and words are moulded there with all the speech muscles working in harmony fully and with economy. One word follows the next, in the moment, formed and sent off. Then the words are forces of power and transformation and are active. In connected Second Circle it is enough to speak clearly because the words are your tools of communication; you are not communicating through the quality of your voice or the signals sent by the patterns of your breath or posture, you are reliant on the power of your words that are connected to you, your thoughts and feelings.

Speech Workout

Keep all the work in place and remember to breathe as it is very common to hold your breath as you concentrate on working your speech muscles.

- The first stage is to open your mouth so that the speech muscles can work. An inactive mouth makes for sloppy speech as the general lack of space makes vigorous and muscular articulation impossible. Not opening your mouth is a common First Circle speech habit. A tight and clenched jaw constricts your speech muscles and can lead to Third Circle fraught and overdone pronunciation.

- Massage the face and gently pull open the jaw.

- Smile and open the jaw without overstretching it and then allow the lips to come together easily and without clenching the teeth.

- Move your tongue around this space, top, bottom and side to side.

- Feel the back of your front teeth.

- Feel the ridge behind the front teeth.

- Tap your tongue on this ridge.

- Notice any difference in the mouth space and the tongue's relationship to that space.

- Now you're going to place the sound forward so that the speech muscles have an optimum chance to mould words.

- Extend your lips forward and vocalize an 'ooh', keeping the jaw released.

- Move 'ooh' into 'moo'.

- With your jaw and mouth released and the sound forward, investigate these consonants. Sound out: M, N, W, L, D, B, V, G.

- If you place your hand on your throat these consonants, if spoken without any vowel sounds ('muh' not 'em'; 'nuh' not 'en' etc.) will still vibrate in your throat as these consonants have voice.

- Keeping your hand on your throat, sound out: P, T, K, F.

- There is no vibration with these sounds as they get their quality from the escaping air in your mouth. These consonants are voiceless.

- Repeat a series of M's and then B's and then P's: M M M M B B B B P P P P.

- Feel the lips meet and part cleanly and with clarity between each sound but not with force or control.

- Speak the following fully without losing the voice quality at the end of each word: Come – Dream – Rub – Scrub – Pop – Drop.

- Repeat a series of W's, bringing the lips forward and releasing the sounds out through the lips: W W W W W.

- Then say the words Water – Wag – Woe.

- Repeat a series of D's and T's: D D D D T T T T.

- Feel the light contact between the tip of your tongue and the ridge behind your top teeth. Make the sound clean but precise with no over friction.

- Try getting to the end of these words, clearly but lightly: Dead – Said – But – Tight – Might.

- Repeat the word 'Lily' a few times, feeling the tongue contact the ridge and move rapidly away from the ridge. Make the tongue work rapidly and feel the word placed fully in the mouth.

- Repeat a series of TH's.

- Feel the tongue move to and away from the back of the upper teeth.

- Get to the end of Birth – Death – Mirth.

- Repeat 'this and that' without your tongue poking out through your teeth.

- Repeat a series of F's and V's. The F is voiceless, the V voiced: F F F F V V V V.

- Feel the top teeth meet the bottom lip cleanly and efficiently and without distorting the lip: Give – Love – Puff – Tough – Off

- Define the word and send it off!

- Repeat a series of G's and K's: G G G G K K K K.

- Keep the mouth released and place the tongue tip behind the bottom teeth in order to stretch the back of your tongue.

- Get to the end of Spark – Dark – Mark – God – Long – Song – Log.

- Define the words but don't dwell on the sounds.

- Repeat a series of words ending in 'ING': Laughing – Singing – Walking – Eating.

- Feel the words at the back of your mouth and a movement there as your soft palate gets working (the soft palate divides the nose from the mouth and air releases down your nose).

- Feel this further by repeating M – N – NG.

- Air is coming down your nose if you are moving the soft palate athletically.

- Move from L as in 'Lily' to L as in 'call'.

- Feel the tongue move from the top on the ridge to the bunching just behind it.

- Get to the end of Call – Wall – Dwell – Bell.

- Repeat a series of R's: R R R R.

- Feel the tongue nearly meet the roof of the mouth (hard palate) and the lips move forward. Speak the words: Right – Round – Romp.

- Repeat a series of S's and Z's: S S S S Z Z Z Z.

- Feel the tongue tip touch the ridge behind your top teeth and the sides touch the sides of the top teeth.

- Get to the end of 'buzz' words: Birds – Herds (these should be sounded as a Z) and then: Shirts – Pumps – Tights (these are S's).

- Avoid pushing this sound, define it gently.

- Rest!

Your jaw, mouth, tongue, lips and soft palate have had a proper workout. I have encouraged you to feel these consonants first but it can be very effective to repeat them all while looking into a mirror – a hand mirror works best. You will then feel the consonants and simultaneously look at how you make them. The ideal visual experience should be one of no facial distortion or overwork. Particularly check that the lips don't purse or pull into a grimace. The mouth should continually move open without pulling back or the jaw clenching. The tongue should move within the confines of your mouth, behind the teeth and with strong and defined movements.

It is usual for the speech muscles to ache after an extended warm-up. As they get stronger and more efficient, this ache dwindles but you can never take clear speech for granted. If you want to be an effective and dynamic speaker you have to work these muscles on a very regular basis.

I want your speech to serve you organically and that can only be possible if these muscles respond unconsciously to your intellectual and emotional needs. I don't want you or your audience to worry about whether you will be clear (First) or whether you are overarticulating to make sure that you are clear (Third). Both positions are barriers between you and your audience.

Practising With Words

There are two common habits of incoherence in speech work. One is forgetting that you have to speak the end of a word and the second is sliding over the syllables in multisyllabic words. Both these habits infuriate the listener as they can't hear important words. It makes correct pacing impossible, it probably means you rush, and it means you cannot convey the true power of a word.

What you say should matter to you, which means you will naturally want to take care to speak clearly. We might not get another chance to speak and as we speak clearly, the physical nature of the clearly spoken word keeps us safe. Clearly defined words are akin to the footholds and handholds on a cliff face – they can keep us safe. Clear speech also makes the audience feel safe.

Remember that during critical moments in life and during important negotiations or dialogues you will probably only get one chance to say what you need to say, so it had better be clear!

- Take a list of multisyllabic words and fully speak them:
    Transformation
    Abundance
    Gratitude

- Speak every physical sound in each word.

- Then speak the words with the appropriate stressed and unstressed syllables.

- The words will now be complete and with their appropriate weight.

The next exercise is one that will be used whenever you are preparing an important speech. I have spoken about the dance of muscles that occurs in your mouth as you speak. A great dancer works out every step in order to dance freely and organically in front of an audience, never taking their body's responses for granted.

This attitude is often lacking in speakers. Most of us take speaking too much for granted and consequently fail to prepare our speech muscles with the same diligence. When your speech muscles are well prepared they will serve you well. This preparation cannot be done silently or passively.

Select a well-written extract from a good newspaper, book or poem.

- Go to a wall and gently push against it with one hand.

- Stay breathing and centred.

- Focus in Second Circle to a point just above the eyeline.

- Release an 'ooh' to place your voice.

- Now breathe and mouth the text without using any voice, but feel all the muscles working to form every sound.

- Be particularly diligent when mouthing ends of words and multisyllabic words.

- Read the whole piece in this way.

- When you finish mouthing your extract, go back and read it in full voice.

You will not only be speaking more cleary and in Second Circle but you will understand the extract more fully as the full sound of words actually informs us of their sense.

If you have trouble with the physical make-up of any word or phrase, go back over them, mouthing, until the muscles are educated to make the sounds. Even if you have to take the words to pieces, this is better than standing in front of an audience dreading the imminent arrival of a word in your mouth that you fear you cannot make clearly and might stumble over.

You have taught your muscles the speech dance steps so that they can now work for you, not against you. You are not tripping up or moving over words but are on them and using their power. As you sound the consonants you are connecting in Second Circle to the intellectual presence of the word and therefore can think more clearly.

Take a rest. You have had another speech workout. Your mouth, lips and tongue will be feeling more alive.

The vowels hold the emotional content of words and without consonants they can prove unbearable emotionally, but you need vowels to release the voice and to feel language. This exercise will help you appreciate the harnessing quality of the consonants as they mould sound into word.

- Go back to the wall, resume the push and refocus yourself.

- Keeping the sounds forward, the breath low and the throat open, just speak the vowels of your piece on full voice.

- On finishing this exercise, go back immediately and put in the consonants.

- You will be speaking so clearly and fully!

By now you have experimented and worked on the physical form of words. If you have managed to fully breathe into them you might also have felt their emotional and intellectual power, meaning and content.

Second Circle – Word Connection

Up to now all the work you have done has been to connect your-self to the world. Now you are going to connect with words and their full power and meaning. You have to first know what you want to say and then say it. Great speakers are present with each word as they speak the word. They mean what they say as they say it and therefore language is made concrete. Images are experienced as they are spoken and ideas and feelings are experienced in the word and in the moment a word is spoken.

If the speaker is not experiencing words in the moment and owning these words concretely, the audience cannot fully understand their ideas or passions.

In First Circle, language is experienced from the past. Words are spoken after the experience of the word, idea or feeling. In Third, they are either experienced rapidly or not fully to get to a point in the future, leaving the audience behind and bewildered. Or they are too dwelt upon and overembellished so that the images and ideas have inappropriate weight, which is the verbal equivalent of not being able to see the wood for the trees! In the rush of our lives, speed reading is an attractive option, particularly if you have to plough through acres of debased and irrelevant language. All the rush and bad writing can easily dull your appreciation of language and tire your need to connect with all your presence to the real sound and meaning of a word.

With the work you have done in place, move forward into present and engaged word connection with these exercises.

- Select a reading.

- Look at the words in Second Circle and don't assume

you know what words are there and don't take any word for granted.

- Observe whether you notice any words that you didn't realize were there. You had taken those words for granted.

- Observe whether you fully understand every word.

- You can know a word 'sort of' but not fully know it.

- There can be no 'sort ofs' in good communication. Every word has to be known as fully as you can muster your knowledge of that word.

- Read the piece aloud.

- Try to imagine every word you speak. This will take a lot of time.

- 'Wood' – you have to see the wood.

- 'Trees' – you have to see trees.

- 'Government' – you must have a reaction and find a connection to the word.

- 'Statistic' – you must experience the word to find the connection.

- You might discover you don't know what a word means so you have to look it up in order to make it concrete.

- When you return to read the piece out again with fluency, your connections will be fuller and you will feel more present with words and own them yourself.

- Read the piece again but only reading aloud the words connected to people: names and pronouns.

- Imagine the people as you speak the word.

- Reread it – the people will be more concrete in the reading.

- Repeat the above, reading aloud the other nouns: places, animals, objects.

- Then explore the verbs and feel each activity the verb describes.

- Then explore the adjectives and adverbs.

When you return to fully reading the text you will experience the many words more clearly. You will discover how the connecting words (but, if, and, then) serve your mind. These words move your mind presently through ideas and they are important words but are often forgotten. Bad writing won't survive these exercises as you will immediately notice how redundant and inexpressive many words are.

These word exercises awaken your language imagination and, with exercise, these connections become easier and easier and you become not only clearer but more present with words as you speak.

Pace

Here are the rules that every skilled actor knows. You can speak as fast as you can physically make the words in your mouth and be present with their meaning as you speak them. Pace is reliant on the speaker having athletic speech muscles and clear connection with the meaning of each word as it is spoken.

Pace is also reliant on you being present with your audience and knowing whether they are following and are present with you or not. If you are not present, you can't be aware of their experience of you: aware that you are going too fast and they are lost, confused and bored or aware you are going too slowly and they are lost, confused and bored!

How many times have you as an audience member wanted to shout out, 'You are going too fast,' or 'Get on with it, I'm not stupid.' We all have these savage reactions to the rushers or the plodders who address us.

When you are fully connected physically through your body, breath, voice, speech, words, imagination and emotions to the audience, your presentation will pace itself. When connection to the breath is flowing evenly through the voice, and words are accurately articulated, you will be physically pacing yourself. When your brain and heart are working in tandem with words this working connection will intellectually and emotionally pace you. When your attentiveness to the audience is in Second Circle, that will pace you. When all these factors come together, no-one notices pace. Time becomes pliable and the talk is over too soon. Time has been conquered by the speaker's presence.

You might have had a memory of this, in a presentation either as a speaker or an audience member. It is the ultimate in a powerful exchange that the world seems to stop and all we are conscious of is what is being spoken. You might have experienced this timeless, perfectly paced exchange in intimate conversations with a loved one. This is a complete Second Circle communication, when both parties are equal in giving and taking and there is no jarring break of pace.

However, the problem with the ideal scenario is that you are not conscious of what is going right because you are in the moment and blissfully connected. If you ever ask an actor who has just performed wonderfully what they remember of the performance, they will honestly say, 'Nothing'. They have been so present that they can't tell you how the performance went. We actually learn more when our pace goes wrong and we can use that understanding to get things right and in the moment. When you rush, people can't follow you, they miss words and you have to repeat yourself. An audience will ask a First Circle rusher to repeat themselves; they might be too intimidated to ask a Third Circle rusher to repeat and clarify.

I believe we know when people are not following us. We might not want to address the problem because we don't feel it is our responsibility to pace our words in a way that can be followed. Some of my Third Circle clients have initially expressed a sense that 'If they can't keep up with me it's their fault!' My First Circle clients can have a similar response: 'If they can't come to me and understand me then they are missing out on my knowledge.' And many First Circle speakers have an entrenched view that they have nothing to say that holds any importance so they should get it spoken as quickly as possible. You should know that your rushed communication is uneconomic. Rushing actually wastes time!

Another common misconception to a rusher is that slowing down will be boring. Actually the reverse is true. Rushing is boring, it switches people off faster than anything else. If you look around you, as you rush, people will have picked up your frantic delivery and be fidgeting or doodling but they are not attentive to you and that is why it is inefficient and uneconomic. Your rushed speaking is not getting any results.

If you are a plodder, proceeding at a slow, careful pace, you are probably slowing the energy of the room down in an attempt to spell out information. If this is the case, you are communicating that you don't believe those around you have a high enough intelligence to understand you at a normal pace. Your audience will have urges to hurry you along and even try to finish your thoughts. If they don't behave in this way it is because they are scared of you but they are actually thinking that you are wasting their time.

Remember that the slow evenness of plodders moderates all

passion in a room and locks down inspiration and excitement. It is very controlling and makes the audience feel powerless. A First Circle plodder is progressing with too much care as they are probably unsure of themselves. This unsureness will inevitably be challenged. A First Circle plodder can also be over-reflective and be searching internally for words, and is therefore unaware that the audience is switching off.

A Third Circle plodder is normally relishing their control and also their words and ideas. This comes over as smug and although you might not be challenged you are not liked as a speaker. Plodding wastes time and, as with rushers, both encourage the audience to absent themselves from your words.

Understand the Pause

You might have a good and connected pace but can you pause appropriately and with the right effect?

A pause is effective and very powerful if it is active and in the moment with your intentions and head and heart. Effective pauses include a real pause which is actively searching for the next word or idea. Then there is the pause that actively and truly checks in with the audience. This pause moves through genuine feeling, and helps you to punctuate ideas with real and needed pauses that are filled and required in the effective communication of your presentation.

Ineffective pauses can include a pause for effect ('wasn't that a good point!'), a pause for approval ('I normally get a laugh or an acknowledgement here') and a pause that is a comment and signals what follows in such a way that it undermines the next thought (in theatre we call this one 'acting between the lines'). Then there is the pause to slow you down which is then followed by a rushing of words.

But a pause filled with breath and attention to what you are saying to your audience will give you and your audience a bridge of transitional energy from one idea to another. This creates an exciting pace in any power presentation. You will become aware of pace with the following exercises.

Exercises For Pace and Pause

- Listen out for pace in others — at work, on the radio or television. Identify pace that is too fast or feels too slow.

- Listen for pace that is initially unnoticeable. This is the right pace; it is appropriate and serves the material. This pace is not impeding the structure of the delivery in any way.

- As you listen to the too fast or too slow categories, you will begin to identify that the speaker is disconnected from what they are saying and that they are either in First or Third Circle. When the pace is too fast and they are ahead of connection, the head is ahead and separated from the mouth. When the pace is too slow the speaker is lagging behind in their connections.

- Listen actively to the pauses within pace. Are these pauses suspension that engages you and keeps you present, or are they pauses that stop your concentration and delay the connection or rush it?

- Note how pace and pauses in others affect you, and how you might disengage. As inappropriate pace and pause fragment you, no wonder you get annoyed at the rushers, plodders and pausers.

Now at this point you should listen to yourself and begin to judge your own pace and pausing habits. Record yourself, but bear in mind that most voice recording equipment doesn't give you a true reading of your voice quality and that your voice is richer than the thin sound you might hear as you play yourself back. And as your ears are inside your head, you can't hear yourself as the world does. However, your pace and pausing habits can be accurately and usefully heard.

- Choose a reading or presentation that you might have to read. This could be minutes of a meeting, an introduction, a summary, etc.

- Read your text or one of mine into your recorder.

- Wait at least ten minutes before you play it back as this gives you objectivity.

- Listen to the recording.

- How is your pace and how do you pause?

- If you believe you are too fast, repeat the reading by pushing with one arm on to a wall, breathe low, and take your time to take breath and feel its readiness. Speak 'ooh' to a point above the eyeline and place the voice.

- Read and record again and aim to speak every consonant and the end of every word.

- Pause with breath and thought and only go on when you are ready.

- If you sound too slow, take the above stance with the wall push and breathe low but don't hold the breath, keep breathing fluidly. Place your voice on 'ooh' to a Second Circle point.

- Read and record again.

- This time, speak clearly but don't dwell on words but

move through them and use words to touch and affect the point outside you.

- Repeat with the breath and don't hold the breath as you speak.

- Repeat with a flow of thought and don't block any impulse, so no pause will be overdone and consequently impede meaning or emotion.

- Wait at least ten minutes before listening to the recording and notice differences in your pace and pausing.

- Are the pauses too long, do they stop the action of the reading?

- Are the pauses too short so that we cannot take in the information of the reading?

- Or are your pauses appropriate, giving the listener time to access the previous information and move forward through the pause? An effective pause is filled with energy and doesn't stop a reading, but gives a place of suspension that is active but required as an energized rest before the speaker moves on.

Here are two readings, by Alexander Pope and Thomas Gray. The Pope is written with a fast pace and the Gray with a slow pace. The pace of these readings is embedded into the form of the writing and is the writer's pace when writing.

Breathe and speak both readings aloud. Define each word but allow the ideas and images to flow forward. You might need to read both passages several times, before you are able to judge whether you are going with the pace of each reading or denying the author's pace. Do you think you are holding back or are you unable to speak quickly enough to keep up with the writer's desire? Do you want to move forward and go ahead of the words and consequently not fully speak them?

After several attempts you will begin to speak at the reading's pace, not your own, and then pause with the author's pauses. This workout of pace and pause will eventually enable you to monitor and focus your pace in all your important communications and presentations.

Elegy Written in a Country Churchyard ~ Thomas Gray

The curfew tolls the knell of parting day,
The lowing herd wind slowly o'er the lea,
The ploughman homeward plods his weary way,
And leaves the world to darkness and to me.

Now fades the glimmering landscape on the sight,
And all the air a solemn stillness holds,
Save where the beetle wheels his droning flight,
And drowsy tinklings lull the distant folds;

Save that from yonder ivy-mantled tower
The moping owl does to the moon complain
Of such, as wandering near her secret bower,
Molest her ancient solitary reign.

Beneath those rugged elms, that yew-tree's shade,
Where heaves the turf in many a mouldering heap,
Each in his narrow cell for ever laid,
The rude forefathers of the hamlet sleep.

The breezy call of incense-breathing morn,
The swallow twittering from the straw-built shed,
The cock's shrill clarion, or the echoing horn,
No more shall rouse them from their lowly bed.

For them no more the blazing hearth shall burn,
Or busy housewife ply her evening care;
No children run to lisp their sire's return,
Or climb his knees the envied kiss to share.

Oft did the harvest to their sickle yield,
Their furrow oft the stubborn glebe has broke;
How jocund did they drive their team afield!
How bowed the woods beneath their sturdy stroke!

Let not Ambition mock their useful toil,
Their homely joys, and destiny obscure;
Nor Grandeur hear with a disdainful smile
The short and simple annals of the poor.

The boast of heraldry, the pomp of power,
And all that beauty, all that wealth e'er gave,
Awaits alike the inevitable hour.
The paths of glory lead but to the grave.

Excerpt from An Essay on Criticism ~ Alexander Pope

Of all the causes which conspire to blind
Man's erring judgement, and misguide the mind,
What the weak head with strongest bias rules,
Is pride, the never-failing vice of fools.
Whatever Nature has in worth denied,
She gives in large recruits of needful pride;
For as in bodies, thus in souls, we find
What wants in blood and spirits swelled with wind:
Pride, where wit fails, steps in to our defense,
And fills up all the mighty void of sense.
If once right reason drives that cloud away,
Truth breaks upon us with resistless day.

Trust not yourself: but your defects to know,
Make use of every friend – and every foe.
A little learning is a dangerous thing;
Drink deep, or taste not the Pierian spring.
There shallow draughts intoxicate the brain,
And drinking largely sobers us again.
Fired at first sight with what the Muse imparts,
In fearless youth we tempt the heights of arts,
While from the bounded level of our mind
Short views we take, not see the lengths behind;
But more advanced, behold with strange surprise
New distant scenes of endless science rise!
So pleased at first the towering Alps we try,
Mount o'er the vales, and seem to tread the sky,
The eternal snows appear already past,
And the first clouds and mountains seem the last;
But, those attained, we tremble to survey
The growing labours of the lengthened way,
The increasing prospect tires our wandering eyes,
Hills peep o'er hills, and Alps on Alps arise!

Rhythm

Rhythm is the music and the beat of communication. The music and beat move through the syllables of words and create meaning through stress.

The most obvious speech rhythm is one that follows your heartbeat. De dum, de dum, de dum. This powerful life force of a rhythm is embodied in the English language and meets its greatest exponent in William Shakespeare. It is rather frighteningly called 'iambic' – a word that has sent schoolchildren screaming from rooms for years! No-one invented this rhythm, it is within us all. The heartbeat, the first and last sound we hear. De dum. De dum. De dum.

When you examine this on a deeper level and realize that the 'dum' is a surge of blood travelling through your veins, it will tell you a great deal about rhythms that work positively in the human ear and spirit. On the beat of the 'dum', blood returns energy to the body and that return lifts up the body and voice. This is a life force that is optimistic and flows forward. It is a present and undefeated powerful rhythm.

De Dum – Hello.

If you speak the rhythm of 'de dum' on hello, you sound positive and optimistic, sending the word's energy and rhythm out. It is powerful and affirming.

Speak this poem, 'Ozymandias' by Percy Bysshe Shelley, with breath and allow the 'de dum' to return the rhythm though the words.

*I met a **traveller** from an **antique** land,*
Who said – 'Two vast and trunkless legs of stone.
***Stand** in the **desert**. Near them on the **sand**,*
Half sunk, a shattered visage lies, whose frown
*And wrinkled **lip** and **sneer** of **cold command***
*Tell that its **sculptor** well those **passions read***
Which yet survive, stamped on these lifeless things,
*The **hand** that **mocked** them and the **heart** that **fed**.*
*And on the **pedestal** these **words appear**:*
*'My name is Ozymandias, **King** of **Kings**:*
*Look on my works, ye **mighty**, and despair!'*
Nothing beside remains. Round the decay
Of that colossal wreck, boundless and bare,
*The **lone** and **level sands** stretch **far away**.*

If you speak this poem with its built-in iambic rhythm, you will feel a motor propelling you forward and sense the optimism in the rhythm of the words.

The rhythm of this heartbeat will break and fragment when thoughts and feelings fragment. But the heartbeat returns to the upward driving pulse after fragmentation because the life force of the heartbeat has to go on even after the breaks.

Now experiment with the fashionable rhythm that we all can fall into which is the reverse of the heartbeat and is therefore a life-deadening force when you speak.

This rhythm makes you fall back into First Circle.

Try speaking this poem on DE dum. DE dum.

*I met **a** traveller **from** an antique land,*
*Who said – '**Two** vast and trunkless **legs** of stone*
Stand in the desert. Near them on the sand,
Half sunk, a shattered visage lies, whose frown
And wrinkled lip and sneer of cold command
Tell that its sculptor well those passions read
Which yet survive, stamped on these lifeless things,
The hand that mocked them and the heart that fed.
And on the pedestal these words appear:
'My name is Ozymandias, King of Kings:
Look on my works, ye mighty, and despair!'
Nothing beside remains. Round the decay
Of that colossal wreck, boundless and bare,
The lone and level sands stretch far away.'

The energy is falling away and this fall stops the forward motion of your energy and your life force. It sounds pessimistic and negative and is difficult to listen to and stay attentive to through the spoken energy because it is against the heartbeat.

This fall is mostly First Circle energy but if this rhythm is overstressed, it can be associated with Third Circle *De* dum which is not only pessimistic and negative-sounding but controlling as well!

There is an extension to this rhythm which is the most deadening spoken rhythm. This is the falling line. Here, the speaker might start a thought in Second Circle but, during the thought, trail off into First. There is a dip in the line that can often be observed in the body and head dropping down as the speaker falls off the line. This fall drones on and on with the dying fall of the line, making us all feel sad or even depressed. The overall rhythm sounds so casual that no-one can sustain interest in what is being said as the speaker seems not to care.

Many speakers are aware of the falling line and adopt a technique to shift the rhythm that is equally confusing to the listener. This is the rising line. The end of a thought is forced up but all this does to the rhythm and the sense of the thought is to put a questioning stress on ideas that are not questions. This lift makes statements sound like questions, which gives the listener the sense that the speaker is unsure of what they are saying. Because everything has an upward rhythm, this lift signals weakness and begs interruption. The rhythm is actually saying, 'I don't know what I think and I can't stand by what I say.'

Feel all these rhythms by using either the Shelley poem or your own reading.

Experiment with:

- The falling De dum
- The overstressed falling DE dum
- The falling line
- The rising line

During these experiments you will experience crucial shifts of rhythm in your body, breath and voice. The falling line will be connected to all of you falling and this connection will inevitably pull you away from presence.

In case you are wondering, it takes thousands of hours of training for an actor to be able to play a First Circle character but still communicate powerfully in a space.

Now return to the flowing and natural de dum rhythm of the heartbeat. This rhythm really places your energy into present Second Circle and you should be able to feel the rhythm enter and change your body, breath and voice. If you sense this energy, you can now play with pausing and maintaining presence. An effective pause has to be filled with energy. You should be able to pause and breathe and hold the energy before moving on. The good news is that being in Second Circle takes care of the real rhythm of life and you do it organically. You organically pause and return naturally.

Rhythm, Stress and Meaning

Have you ever heard a speaker overstressing so much that your ear cannot pick out exact meaning? Or have you heard a speaker who has so little stress, definition or rhythm that the meaning flatlines and is also incomprehensible?

There are three main forces that will fully clarify your communication.

1. Correct and clear pronunciation
2. Specific intellectual meaning
3. Intense emotional connection

Stress is within the rhythm of what you say and is released through the syllables in the words. A stressed syllable gives words their pronunciation and heavily stressed words within a thought define both meaning and emotion. To fulfil the power of a stressed syllable, you need unstressed syllables. This process is so natural to you that when you are happy and not threatened, it all works nicely and stress works with meaning, but it could all get tangled up when you are under threat and are losing your presence.

The unstressed syllable is the 'de' in 'de dum' and when an unstressed syllable appears in language the vowel within the syllable becomes shortened or, more accurately, neutralized. The neutralized vowel is a short 'er' sound.

This system of unstressed and weighted syllables is how you learn to pronounce a word. The short 'er' is not the sound in the word 'early' but the shortened sound at the end of the word 'Mother'. A mispronunciation of 'mother' would be 'moth*er*', both syllables having the same weight.

'Today' is not stressed with equal stress – 'to-day' – but 'ter-day'. De-dum.

Dispute is not 'dis-pute' but 'des-pute'.

Tomorrow is not 'to-morrow' but 'ter-morrow'.

The robots in children's TV stress every syllable and that communication can only be listened to for a few moments before it tangles and confuses your brain.

Sometimes we have to shake our heads to understand the too-weighted stress of a foreigner speaking English or someone wrongly stressing a word and making it sound foreign.

If in doubt as to how to pronounce a word, look in a good dictionary and the word is phonetically displayed and the stressed syllables are preceded by stress signs – 'to´day'. Even if you cannot read phonetics you can observe the right stress and pronounce a word accurately.

Don't worry if certain stresses are not in your accent. The relevance of pronunciation and stress is to aid the general audience in identifying a word and if you overstress (Third Circle) you will not only jar the ear of your audience but reduce every-day words to alien sounds. The First Circle habit of too-even stressing flattens words out to such an extent that we can't be bothered to listen as there is no coherent texture or stressed signal to help us understand what is being communicated.

Stress gives agreed pronunciation but also defines exact meaning within a thought.

Now remember the neutralization of vowels within unstressed syllables for pronunciation, because you now have to go further. You must examine the slight neutralization of syllables that elicits meaning through specific communication even if the pronunciation requires a syllable to be stressed.

In order to define meaning in your thoughts you have to neutralize certain words – including their stressed syllables within phrases or thoughts.

Let's examine 'that man'. If the man is a passing reference to a man, say in a thought like, 'that man said he would go and get my luggage,' the 'that' would be neutralized and the letter 'a' in 'that' moves towards 'thert'. However, if you were a victim of crime and were looking at men in an identity parade, you would stress '*that* man' giving full weight to the 'a' in 'that'.

Obviously, if you know what you are saying you would naturally stress and neutralize vowels to clarify your exact meaning.

Experiment with this sentence:

'Today my mother is coming here for supper.'

A flowing and evenly stressed delivery would communicate the whole meaning of this sentence.

This delivery would be well balanced without any stress that might shade the meaning or give it a weightier agenda. The delivery gives us information without the speaker giving the delivery specific texture of meaning.

In this way, evenly weighted speakers can be criticized for not exposing their preferences to ideas or having emotional connection to the information.

Of course, this well-balanced delivery has to be taught to speakers who must be objective and impersonal. For instance, good newsreaders should deliver in this way, giving the audience the information without giving a personal opinion. Less effective newsreaders can actually apply stress in a way that gives their prejudice to a news story.

Now let us get personal and more connected through stress.

Again, take the sentence, 'Today my mother is coming here for supper.'

Now, if you stress 'mother' in this sentence and consequently move towards neutralizing the other words, the sentence's meaning changes texture and specificity.

The meaning is 'mother' is coming, not someone else. The person you are speaking to could be your brother who is expecting your father to attend, not your mother.

As the word 'mother' takes on this weight, the musical rhythm or inflection of the sentence changes. The inflections move up through 'today my', land on 'mother' and fall through 'is coming here for supper'.

Now play the same game and stress 'today'. Here the meaning is not tomorrow or next week. The inflection moves down from 'today' through the rest of the sentence.

A stress on 'my' indicates 'not your mother' and the upward and falling inflections rise and fall around 'my'.

Continue with a stress on 'here' and the meaning indicates not at your house, at a restaurant or at her house, but 'here'.

'Supper' stressed implies not breakfast, lunch, tea or drinks.

This is all obvious, until it goes wrong when a mis-stress can put you in a terrible position, communication misinformation, or even cause a diplomatic disaster. Mis-stress often happens with nerves. It can happen when a speech is read but not fully prepared or prepared aloud, is not fully understood or its real context known.

Speakers that understress (First Circle) or overstress (Third Circle) under pressure and are ill-prepared can make a nonsense of even very simple words and ideas.

Emotion in the voice is in the vowels, so the vowels in words that contain your emotion gain more weight. This emotional vowel weight will shift rhythm and stress within sentences, weighting words and vowels in order to express feelings.

Take the last sentence. If the speaker hated or was frightened of their mother, the word mother would contain movement and weight through the vowels in mother, expressing the feelings towards the mother.

If you were appalled at her arrival 'here', for whatever reason, then the 'ere' would change weight and length to signal the shock of mother *here*.

Understanding these nuances of stress and their connection to the weight of voice enables you to communicate very personal connections through your rhythm, stress and the accompanying inflections. A good Second Circle speaker must use pause, rhythm, stress and inflections to communicate their full present authenticity. I recently worked with a leader who communicated clearly through intellectual stress but appeared, in the words of one of his colleagues, 'as hard as an assassin'. His actual warmth emerged not only with the opening of his voice but with a more flowing rhythm and full inflections. The opposite of that problem was the leader who sounded over-emotional under pressure and consequently incoherent. She indulged too much in personal connections and one of her colleagues was overheard by her saying, 'She's not going to cry again is she?' Actually, the content of her presentations was well written and rational and with work on clear stress and rhythm, the meaning emerged and balanced with her personal connections making her a fine speaker.

Let us put all these natural and basic speech components together by returning to Shelley.

If you follow the rhythm of his writing, based on the iambic, and allow for the breaks in his rhythm to clarify meaning, you will give a clear but impersonal communication of this sonnet.

- To do this, gently hum the sonnet standing in Second Circle, breathing and voicing forward. Come back to speaking it with the energy and pause you found when humming. The hum is actually allowing your voice to meet Shelley's voice through his rhythms, stresses and pauses.

- Now let me conduct you through the lines. As you speak, stress these words:

    I met a **traveller** from an **antique** land,
    Who said – 'Two vast and trunkless legs of stone
    Stand in the **desert**. Near them on the **sand**,
    Half sunk, a shattered visage lies, whose frown
    And wrinkled **lip** and **sneer** of **cold command**
    Tell that its **sculptor** well those **passions read**
    Which yet survive, stamped on these lifeless things,
    The **hand** that **mocked** them and the **heart** that **fed**.
    And on the **pedestal** these **words appear**:
    'My name is Ozymandias, **King** of Kings:
    Look on my works, ye mighty, and despair!'
    Nothing beside remains. Round the decay
    Of that colossal wreck, boundless and bare,
    The **lone** and **level sands** stretch **far away**.

- Some of these stresses might work for you, others annoy you.

- That annoyance is good because you are forming an opinion of what you want to convey or feel. Read it again with your rhythm and stresses. Now you are serving Shelley's overall intention but also adding your own intellectual and emotional connections.

This work is essential when you speak other people's words. You have to examine the writer's intentions through stress and rhythm and then make your own connections with the writing, otherwise the words you speak won't sound like you. You will create a distance between your voice and the writer's voice.

It is possible that you have written a speech that you are preparing to deliver but have written it in a style or language that is not really your own speaking style.

Examine the speech aloud and with the same care.

Stress for sense and then connect through the ideas and images to make the language and presentation personal.

The more you can speak great writing aloud, the more you will realize that there is nothing random in powerful expression – the rhythm and stress are part of the text and expose the text's meaning and its heart.

Summary

- Your voice is given clarity and emotional resonance through good articulation and clear speech, a skill learned and honed through regular practice.

- Good speech preparation is not silent or passive – harness the power of language by feeling each consonant and vowel as it leaves your mouth.

- Pacing is crucial to speech – pauses, rhythm and stress all give meaning to language and are vital tools to convey your message.

STRUCTURE

No formal presentation, interview, negotiation or conversation should be planned or contemplated without working on clear structures. Think of structure as scaffolding that holds your thoughts and feelings and focuses them into Second Circle. As you become familiar with structure, you will be able to break out of the formal scaffolding at will and return to the form when necessary. In other words you won't ramble if challenged and you will be able to divert from the roadway if extra information in any discussion is required, and get back to the road or point when required.

Simply put, the main purpose of speaking in Second Circle is to take yourself and others somewhere! In First you can actually move backwards in your thinking and speak about something relevant to you but not to others and consequently lose and confuse the audience. Or you can stay stuck on a point, repeating it endlessly as though others haven't understood the point. In Third you can move so rapidly forward that the audience can't keep up with any structure because they haven't been taken along a road but straight to the end of the journey without being shown the way.

In Second, you are present with and allow each word and thought to be actively moving you forward. When a diversion is necessary you will move away from the planned road, deal with what is off the road, and return to the exact location of departure and proceed as previously planned.

The structural map I am describing is not new. It is very old. Until a few years ago, every child at school was taught to think and write in this way. Many of you know these structures but sometimes don't apply them enough in formal communication. These structures have been termed Classical Thought, and every writer wrote with these structures, until deconstruction in the early twentieth century smashed up the road. I have taught business leaders and politicians who have not had the advantages of being taught Classical Thought. They are brilliant at what they do but have found that less brilliant colleagues can out-debate them with this crucial structure. However, once learnt and mastered, they have been able to hold their own with all their classically educated peers.

So what is Classical Thought? It is a sequential journey that moves forward and builds an argument and seeks, through the argument, a resolve. You simply open up a debate and ask a question. You explore and journey through all the possibilities of the question and actively move towards a resolution, the journey's end. There is order in a classical journey. You might not know where you are going but you know you have to move forward from a problem and examine every stage of the problem and possibly discover other problems along the way until you reach a resolution or conclusion.

Sometimes journeys aren't neat and tidy, sometimes you have to start at the end and work backwards or reflect on each discovery on the journey. However the Classical structure has to be used and understood if you are to be a successful speaker.

From this base you can move off in all sorts of directions securely and take your audience with you.

The notion of Classical Thought, even the word 'Classical', can frighten off many people, but let me suggest something exciting. These structures are old and I am now going to suggest that they are so old that they gave us the thought patterns that allowed the human race to evolve and dominate the planet. They are what make us human and not apes, as you can see in these sentences:

- 'The tracks are moving in the direction of the waterhole, therefore the deer has gone to the waterhole.'

- 'If I bind my flint axehead on to this stick, I can kill the buffalo from a distance and avoid being killed or injured.'

- 'My mother has died so I will bury her with her favourite utensils. She will need them in the afterlife.'

Those three examples of Neolithic thought patterns are no different in structure to Shakespeare's 'To be or not to be: that is the question.' These structures are found in well-written recipes. You couldn't make the dish without them, because if the carrot goes into the stew at the wrong time it doesn't get cooked! It is found in well-written instruction manuals; if it is not in those manuals you are driven mad trying to put together the flatpack bookshelf. It is the structure used by a judge summing up a case or by a barrister interrogating a witness.

- 'Please go back to the beginning of your story.'

- 'You've made that point, please move forward in the story.'

- 'Do you conclude that you saw the accused at the bar on Sunday 3rd October 1985?'

This structure is so embedded in our beings that we devise toys for our children to awaken and understand it. Dolls within dolls, boxes within boxes. The child has to open one doll to get to the next doll which is the same as having to start at the beginning of a story before you can get to the end.

When these structures are awakened and secured within you, you will be free to check in with your audience, leave the presentation and look at the audience, take a difficult question that is designed to knock you sideways, and still return to your structure, your journey.

There are three basic scenarios you should practise.

The Planned Speech and Journey

When you write a speech or plan a presentation you should start with scaffolding your ideas.

- Where do I start? How do I open the debate?

- What points should be cited and explored?

- Where am I going?

- What is my resolve?

Within this process you must initially be brutal about irrelevant ideas or material. Any random words or ideas should be pruned until you have your strong, clear directions in place.

Once the structure is firm you can divert, tell a joke or a personal story, safely and relevantly.

Try this exercise.

- Describe a known but complex actual journey. It could be your journey to work every day or the one you take to visit a parent or friend.

- Speak it aloud.

- Describe it clearly and thoroughly and as though the person hearing the directions must take this journey now and urgently. They must not get lost as the welfare of one of your loved ones is dependent on them completing the journey successfully. After this exercise go back over the journey and make sure all the necessary details are there; if they are there then the scaffolding is in place.

- Now describe the same journey in a more relaxed

way, making it as colourful as you can, maybe remembering and describing an interesting character or event you encountered once on the journey. You are still structuring your journey but making it more personal and interesting.

The clear trap a First Circle thinker can fall into is giving all the personal details and reactions without the muscle and vigour of the structured journey. The Third Circle trap is to know the journey so well that you can't be bothered to take anyone else along with you.

- Now, imagine you are defending a close friend. They have been wrongly accused of a minor crime. You weren't with them at the time of the crime but have five concrete reasons why they couldn't have committed it.

- At this stage, don't be personal or emotional. Explain the facts clearly and conclude with a reason why they are not guilty.

- Now flesh this defence with any personal or passionate details as you defend your friend.

Now go to a problem that you face in your workplace: a problem you know how to solve, even if no-one has asked you to solve the problem.

- Prepare what you are going to say in this way.

- Start with speaking the problem and then list all the factors of the problem, describing the solutions and concluding with the action that should immediately be taken.

- Imagine, in this preparation, all the objections your colleagues will raise and make sure you have information to defend your point of view.

When you have completed these tasks you have begun to develop your structure muscles which will now be put to the test.

The Unprepared Speech or an Unexpected Question

A sense of structure has to be so embedded in you that you can think presently and improvise in the moment, taking yourself and others on a clear, forward-moving journey and reaching a conclusion.

This is how Shakespeare's characters speak, under duress. His speeches are not planned but are passionate journeys seeking a safe home and conclusion. The more you practise these structures, the freer you will be in exploring everyday exchanges and presenting them with structure.

Read aloud Shakespeare's famous speech from *Hamlet* in Second Circle. You will definitely notice how each thought takes you forward and structures Hamlet's quest in the way you have been practising. Also notice how each thought is moving forward and discovering many ideas. The first line, 'To be, or not to be; that is the question:' has three discoveries in that one line. You have to be present and in the moment with each discovery to make it work and concrete. Also notice how each thought builds from the last one. There is no intellectual withdrawal or drooping into First Circle or forcing into Third Circle. Each thought is a rung on a ladder taking Hamlet to his eventual conclusion.

To be, or not to be; that is the question:
Whether 'tis nobler in the mind to suffer

The slings and arrows of outrageous fortune,
Or to take arms against a sea of troubles,
And, by opposing, end them? To die, to sleep;
No more; and, by a sleep to say we end
The heart-ache and the thousand natural shocks
That flesh is heir to, 'tis a consummation
Devoutly to be wish'd. To die, to sleep;
To sleep: perchance to dream: ay, there's the rub;
For in that sleep of death what dreams may come
When we have shuffled off this mortal coil,
Must give us pause. There's the respect
That makes calamity of so long life;
For who would bear the whips and scorns of time,
The oppressor's wrong, the proud man's contumely,
The pangs of dispriz'd love, the law's delay,
The insolence of office, and the spurns
That patient merit of the unworthy takes,
When he himself might his quietus make
With a bare bodkin? Who would fardels bear,
To grunt and sweat under a weary life,
But that the dread of something after death,
The undiscover'd country from whose bourn
No traveller returns, puzzles the will,
And makes us rather bear those ills we have
Than fly to others that we know not of?
Thus conscience does make cowards of us all;
And thus the native hue of resolution
Is sicklied o'er with the pale cast of thought,
And enterprises of great pitch and moment
With this regard their currents turn awry,
And lose the name of action. Soft you now!
The fair Ophelia! Nymph, in thy orisons
Be all my sins remember'd.

Here is a modern example of a wonderfully constructed and executed speech – it is well worth seeking out a recording of Barack Obama delivering this speech to see effective and powerful presentation in action. Notice the structure, rhythm and stresses throughout that give power to the words.

I was never the likeliest candidate for this office. We didn't start with much money or many endorsements. Our campaign was not hatched in the halls of Washington – it began in the backyards of Des Moines and the living rooms of Concord and the front porches of Charleston.

It was built by working men and women who dug into what little savings they had to give five dollars and ten dollars and twenty dollars to this cause. It grew strength from the young people who rejected the myth of their generation's apathy; who left their homes and their families for jobs that offered little pay and less sleep; from the not-so-young people who braved the bitter cold and scorching heat to knock on the doors of perfect strangers; from the millions of Americans who volunteered, and organized, and proved that more than two centuries later, a government of the people, by the people and for the people has not perished from this Earth. This is your victory.

I know you didn't do this just to win an election and I know you didn't do it for me. You did it because you understand the enormity of the task that lies ahead. For even as we celebrate tonight, we know the challenges that tomorrow will bring are the greatest of our lifetime – two wars, a planet in peril, the worst financial crisis in a century. Even as we stand here tonight, we know there are brave Americans waking up in the deserts of Iraq and the mountains of Afghanistan to risk their lives for us. There are mothers and fathers who will lie awake after their children fall asleep and wonder how they'll make the mortgage, or pay their doctor's bills, or save enough for college. There is new energy to harness and new jobs to be created; new schools to build and threats to meet and alliances to repair.

The road ahead will be long. Our climb will be steep. We may not get there in one year or even one term, but America – I have never been more hopeful than I am tonight that we will get there. I promise you – we as a people will get there.

There will be setbacks and false starts. There are many who won't agree with every decision or policy I make as President, and we know that government can't solve every problem. But I will always be honest with you about the challenges we face. I will listen to you, especially when we disagree. And above all, I will ask you join in the work of remaking this nation the only way it's been done in America for two hundred and twenty-one years – block by block, brick by brick, calloused hand by calloused hand.

What began twenty-one months ago in the depths of winter must not end on this autumn night. This victory alone is not the change we seek – it is only the chance for us to make that change. And that cannot happen if we go back to the way things were. It cannot happen without you.

So let us summon a new spirit of patriotism; of service and responsibility where each of us resolves to pitch in and work harder and look after not only ourselves, but each other. Let us remember that if this financial crisis taught us anything, it's that we cannot have a thriving Wall Street while Main Street suffers – in this country, we rise or fall as one nation; as one people.

Interviews, Meetings, Negotiations, Conversations and Confrontations

The last scenario is probably the most common one you will encounter in your professional life. It is also the hardest and your success at it is reliant on you practising with structure. It is actually easier to speak *Hamlet* and stay on the structural journey than to steer others and reach a resolution. It takes skill to steer others and requires you to walk over glass or balance on a tightrope. You can only succeed in steering others if you are structured and in Second Circle with everyone. It is essential that you stay in a give-and-take relationship with everyone present. In this way, you listen and learn from everyone and develop ideas and resolutions together.

A Third Circle leader can run a meeting, a negotiation, an interview, etc. with all structures in place but not allowing intervention and thus making everyone in the room feel redundant. These exchanges are non-exchanges and important information and insights sometimes unspoken are lost to the meeting. Leaders who operate in this way might as well be in a meeting on their own.

A First Circle leader in these situations will allow the structures to be overwhelmed and lost. An enormous amount of time is wasted as the backward energy of First Circle cannot focus the group, enabling chaos to rule and if a conclusion is reached it might be without all the information fully examined.

The give and take of Second Circle allows others to contribute, and the structures and journey of thought mean that the flow and resolve of the meeting is fully pursued.

I have come across many entrepreneurs who, from an early age, have had such brilliant business ideas that seem so obvious to them that they have never bothered to structure these ideas in language. In fact, some of them started creating businesses so early that they left formal education early. This inability to structure ideas and form language to communicate ideas means that at some point they clash with colleagues who seem to them stupid, as they don't understand the obvious. Actually, these people have not been exposed to structured thinking or a basic explanation of what is going on in the entrepreneur's mind. You cannot expect people to understand or be present to your ideas if you don't structure them.

Summary

- Think of structure as a journey – a properly drawn roadmap will allow for detours, for spontaneity, but also allow you to get back on track with ease.

- Decide where you are going on your journey, establish a clear outline and then personalize it with description and colour.

- Imagine and explore any pitfalls along the way – anticipate problems and have a plan for resolving them.

LISTENING

Present listening is as essential to your survival and power as breathing. I admit you don't die if you don't listen accurately but you do miss out on the world, the people in the world, and what is happening around you.

Apart from anything else, if you don't listen in Second Circle you will be oblivious to those who wish you harm, you will hurt those you care about and miss every positive opportunity presented to you by others.

First Circle Listeners

First Circle listeners tend to hear everything through their own needs. You hear only what you need to hear, not the complete communication. In this way you can miss the point or take something too personally and out of balance. I have often given very positive feedback to a First Circle listener but they only hear the one negative comment amongst the twenty positive ones.

Most of us have had those deeply frustrating experiences when addressing a First Circle listener. When you speak to a First Circle listener, you get the clear impression that they leave you and glaze over. They are somewhere else and not with you all of the time. You can feel ignored or unimportant to them. If you are a leader and listen in First Circle, you will appear rude, dismissive and uncaring. You are probably also very lonely as most people will have given up trying to make contact with you. You might only realize this, as a client did, when he started to lose his best staff who were fed up at all their brilliance falling on deaf ears.

Third Circle Listeners

Third Circle listeners get impatient. They are ahead of all communication, and act as if they know what you are going to say before you say it. They can even finish your sentences. They listen for the general point but will often miss the detail of what you say.

If you are a Third Circle listener you will lose good staff as they get tired of being shouted down and will feel undervalued and unappreciated.

Much of our inability to listen well in Second Circle is that the world is bombarding us with irrelevant intrusive static sound. There is so much noise out there that we have to close down and withdraw. In a way we are living in a Third Circle world assaulting our ears with generalized noise pollution.

Learning to Listen

Rather than specific exercises I am about to suggest simple shifts of practice in listening to 'prick up your ears'.

- On a regular basis, practise trying to experience silence. Nowhere is completely silent but time spent seeking silence and being silent yourself in quiet places will help your ears return to their natural sensitivity.

- In silence, lie on the floor or sit upright and pick out sounds around you.

- You are now listening in Second Circle. When you are accustomed to this silence, play some favourite music on a low volume. Your ears will stretch towards the sound, heightening your listening.

- Notice how you listen to people that interest you. Stay in Second and really appreciate what they are saying.

- Check that your listening doesn't wander off into First or Third Circle. You will begin to understand that you can call your attention back and might even recapture your attention by shifting your body and breath into Second Circle.

- One of the signs you will see in many people as they switch off is when they hold their breath or do not breathe to you.

- Keep breathing and you have a chance to keep listening.

- Now practise staying in Second as you listen to those

who annoy you, don't respect you or feel superior to you. This will be a huge struggle but you will learn a lot about yourself and those around you.

- The people who you normally don't listen to will be thrilled and you will find out important insights into them. This will give you more strategies in dealing with negative forces and you will begin to make strong alliances through listening with positive force.

Summary

- Focused, attentive listening is a skill that many people have lost, but that can give you tremendous advantages if practised regularly

- Silence is a wonderful aid to developing listening skills – seek it out whenever possible

You now have enough knowledge and craft to work on most challenges you will meet. The tools of the trade – body, breath, voice , speech, structure and listening – are available to improve your form and delivery. These are the areas you need to work on when you identify that you are not present when you speak.

You might already know your strengths and weaknesses but it is probable that in some challenges you will need to focus on your presence in both your form and content.

If you believe that your content is not being communicated, then you need to work on words and structures. You must always identify for yourself why you are speaking and what you want to achieve as you speak.

After coaching thousands of speakers I would say you can never do enough work on your breath – when I have had to deal swiftly with a terrified speaker, release of shoulder tension with a low-realm breath is essential to give them a fighting chance.

Now that you are armed with practical skills, in the next section we will look at the common challenges to effective communication you may face.

3 Challenges

STRESS AND FEAR

The worst thing you can do with any stress or fear is not recognize it! This denial is very possible if you are bluffing in Third or hiding from it in First. You have to know that stress and fear can be massive blocks in any attempt to communicate. You have to recognize your fears and the blocks they create in order to successfully stay present and powerful through these emotions.

Symptoms of Stress and Fear

The general manifestations of stress and fear appear in the body, breath and voice in the following ways.

A habitual First Circle presenter experiences a great implosion of energy – the emotions attack you, shrinking the body, shortening the breath and reducing the voice. This implosion of energy can make you shake. All that can occur before you even start to speak. You swallow words, rush and become muddled. You forget thoughts or where the idea is going. Your listening becomes self-critical.

Specific physical symptoms include tight and pulled round shoulders, a gripping sensation in the upper chest, the jaw tightening and difficulty in swallowing. The head might pull down with a locking of the spine and knees. The stomach might ache and, if held tight, it stops any breath going down into the abdominal area, which is your reservoir of power. As the panic increases, the body becomes so taut that breath can only fill your upper chest. You can feel that you might pass out. The whole audience will know that a First Circle speaker is petrified.

The Third Circle manifestation of stress and fear is generally a feeling of the body about to explode. The body seems to move off the ground and braces itself for a blow on the chin. The breath is drawn in forcibly and with noise, the voice can become too loud and insistent, the speaking too precise, the thinking can get stuck on one point and listening to yourself can become so controlling that any interruption can be drowned by vocal volume. Specifically, the shoulders and upper chest rise up and the head gets pulled back with the teeth clenched, the spine can actually be painful with rigid bracing, the breath blocked into the ribcage, the stance too wide and the pelvic area forward. After speaking the voice could feel scratchy and tired. Many members of an audience will not know a Third Circle speaker is nervous but will experience a loud insensitivity. Many of my Third Circle clients who have been fearful in a presentation lash out inappropriately at remarks from the audience, unaware that they are hurting people, and are shocked when they are rebuked later for the lash.

The awful truth about stress and fear is that it is unattractive to others. Your distress and pain are an enormous turn-off to the world. Even the sweetest spirits can appear to be distasteful if fear overwhelms them. In First Circle you appear weak, self-conscious, passive-aggressive, manipulative or self-indulgent. In Third, fear communicates a bully, aggression, insensitivity and arrogance.

The task is to know you will be stressed and fearful but to apply your technical skills and not allow the effects to pull you out of Second Circle presence! As you recognize where and how your fear and stress grip you, then you have a chance to move through these tensions and stay present in and with the world. The most positive quality of being in Second Circle is that you are focused outside yourself and worrying about others and not yourself, which can immediately diminish stress and fear.

Knowing Your Enemies

To be conscious of your habits with fear and stress, you have to be in Second Circle. This is hard because the first thing fear and stress does is chase your presence away or put you into a presence of fight or flight, which is equally unhelpful. To combat stress and fear and their impact on you we are going to work gently and in two ways.

1. You must work on yourself as subtly as possible and notice the body's nuances accurately, but also recognize the habit as it first appears.
2. You must meet these enemies outside the fearful and stressful situation of professional presentation.

I am going to encourage you to examine what stress and fear trigger in you while you are in a safe place. These small triggers will give you an accurate understanding of where and how these small physical triggers can explode or implode under pressure.

Although stress and fear have similar physical manifestations, stress is a trickier animal to identify as it creeps into us more insidiously and can take years before its full-blown effects are experienced. Fear is more immediate and its power on you unavoidable. Understanding the effects of fear gives you an understanding of your stress patterns. You might already be aware of the large and general effects of your fear but you have to learn to identify the first subtle signs: the primary triggers which, when understood, can be released in order to keep you in Second Circle.

Memory Trigger Exercise

- Have a notebook and pen ready to record any physical triggers.

- Lie on your back with your calves resting on a chair and your thighs released at right angles to the floor. You are adopting the deep release position.

- Be comfortable and safe. Have a small cushion under your head and be in a space where you won't be disturbed.

- Breathe calmly, slowly and deeply.

- Do this until you feel your whole body release into the floor, chest stilled and open, shoulders open, jaw unclenched.

- The breath must be fluid in and out without holds, the ribcage moving gently but fully. The abdominal area should be allowing a full movement of the breath down into the groin area.

- Enjoy this position and then be aware of all your body and breath rhythms with a Second Circle mind on yourself.

- Check all through your body and breath, note and release any holds.

- Stay in this position until you feel centred and safe.

- Now, with full Second Circle concentration and focus,

visit in your memory any events or people that you connect to fear.

- You might not need an aid, but if you do, here are some common memories:
    - Speaking in public
    - Loss or death
    - Humiliation
    - Failure
    - Loneliness

- Try to be as concrete as possible in your memory.

- Return to an examination of your body and breath.

- Has anything shifted? Can you observe any tensions in your body, and breath and if so where they are?

- Try to isolate any patterns of physical tensions and breath holds and rhythms.

- Write down any observations.

- Return to being relaxed.

- Now visit the present and check on any fears you have now.

- Observe whether there are any shifts in your body and breath and where they are.

- Write down any shifts.

- Repeat the process and visit fears in the future.

- Roll over and slowly get into a Second Circle centred standing position. You might have to walk around the room or push against a wall to re-engage yourself.

- In the standing position, revisit any memory of fear that

created the most vivid reaction in you and note how that manifests itself. These consequences could be very small, and include a slight shifting back or pushing forward through the body, or adjustments in the jaw, neck and shoulders, spine, stomach or knees. They might be very small tensions but remember these slight shifts can be debilitatingly multiplied hugely under pressure and can trigger a series of reactions that can immobilize you.

- Repeat the process in a seated position, checking and noting if you find yourself shuffling in your seat, fidgeting and tightening.

- Collate all your findings and you will have a physical and breath map of your fear.

When you're ready you can repeat the experience to map out your stress patterns.

- Starting from the floor position, search for memories that stress you. These could be:
    Money worries
    Too much to do in too little time
    Pressures of travel – driving in jams
    Missing trains
    Broken technology
    Inefficient work colleagues
    Children
    Arguments with family, etc.

- Take yourself into the present and future with these threats to your wellbeing.

- Focus on any physical and breath shifts. Do they occur in the same vicinities and ways that fear gripped you?

- Take notes.

- Standing and sitting stress patterns might initially be less obvious except you might find a general distress in your body, but try to find the key place. This is only possible if you are in Second Circle with yourself.

- By now you have a list of physical and breath symptoms to address when frightened or stressed. You are beginning to know your enemies and can now plan strategies to disarm reactions that disempower you.

Strategies

Examine your list. You have experienced a sequence of symptoms through three physical positions – lying, standing and sitting. You now must place lying, standing and sitting into separate columns and ask these two questions.

1. What happens first in lying, standing and sitting?
2. What had the most impact on your distress in each of these positions? Your breath, shoulders, abdominal area, etc.

In the 'lying' list you might have noticed that you first hold your breath, followed by your shoulders lifting and jaw clenching. In the standing and sitting lists, these symptoms might be different or the same. Now you are beginning to know what starts the physical and breath disempowerment and where it travels in your body and breath.

By the end of this list-making you will have the beginnings of a real knowledge of your physical and breath enemies. This process is not an exact science because the complexity of fear and stress is reliant on so many changing factors, which is why you have to stay so alert and present to all possible reactions. What you will have is a growing understanding of a series of possible blocks in your power, how you can address them as and when they occur.

The next stage becomes a preparation in the world. You must search for events in your daily life – actually seek them – that you know could make you fearful or stressed.

- You might volunteer to speak at a meeting that scares you.

- You might question a colleague who scares you.

- You might perform a task that stresses you, or harder, you might not move away from a person that scares you when they enter your space.

These events can be low key, and in some ways the low-key ones help you understand the subtle changes in your body better than the heated events. Don't feel that I am asking you to put yourself in danger but I am suggesting you have to risk some stress and fear to practise strategies because this work does take practice.

As you live and are present in any of these events you consciously adjust tensions and breath.

Your strategies could go like this:

- 'My knees are locking – unlock them.'

- 'My shoulders are creeping up – release them.'

- 'I've stopped breathing – breathe.'

- 'My breath is getting shallow – breathe deeply.'

- 'My body is pulling back – I'll stay present and forward.'

These strategies are simple but effective and they begin to become organic. Your natural state will be an ally for you as the body and breath want to stay natural and are relieved that you are helping them to do so. You want to survive and you will be overjoyed that you can survive stress and fear. I don't underestimate the courage that some of this will take; consequently you must give yourself permission to withdraw from a situation if need be. However, when you sense that you can monitor your body and breath in these smaller events and stay in Second, you are ready for the bigger and more fearful scenes. No two meetings between you and fear will be the same but you will begin to control responses and stay present.

Facing the Fear of Presenting

I am going to take you through an imagined event, speaking to an audience of 200 on a platform and behind a lectern. You have prepared your presentation and warmed up your body, breath and voice.

- Before the event you visit the space.

- Stand and breathe from the place where you will make your entrance.

- Imagine your fear and regulate your breath.

- Find a wall that can be pushed against to re-engage any panic in the breath.

- Practise walking on to the platform in Second Circle.

- Practise breathing the space as you walk on.

- Practise reaching the lectern and standing in Second

Circle beside the lectern. Can you push and breathe on the lectern? Experiment to see if you can.

- Breathe the space and calm the breath.

- Practise walking off in Second Circle.

- If you are using notes or technology, practise with breath reading from the notes and working the technology.

- At the start of the event, stand in the wings and breathe as low and as calmly as possible.

- Regulate any tensions and release them.

- Push against a wall and breathe if you begin to panic.

- As you walk on, connect by breathing the space with the audience.

- Make eye contact with the audience.

- Don't rush. Arrive at the lectern and stand comfortably and look at the audience, continually breathing.

- Any tensions that you feel in your shoulders, jaw, knees, resolve before starting to present.

- Make sure the notes are in place before starting.

You have done everything possible in your preparation to keep your fear at bay, but you also have to know that fear can grip mid-event. If you start well then you might not look back but fly with a positive use of adrenalin, but it doesn't always happen like that. Be prepared for fear to grip you at any time – at the first sign of breathlessness or physical tensions take immediate action. Obviously mid-event fear is initiated by something not going to plan. Technology breaking down, a muddle of notes, an awkward question, a negative audience, etc. The simple trick is to never move out of Second Circle, never think you are home and dry until the very end of the presentation, never comment on a mistake but cancel and continue through the mistakes. No presentation is perfect and the truth is that any live event can trip you up and lead to problems. As Hamlet says, 'the readiness is all'.

I haven't yet discussed your voice or speech under stress, mainly because if you can stay physically in Second Circle and breathe fully then your voice stays connected when under pressure. If you have noticed that your voice shakes, goes up in pitch or seems to get stuck under pressure then you need to stop, take breath and open your throat by thinking of a yawn. These strategies will open the voice and can be performed so subtly that your audience won't notice that you are reconnecting yourself.

You must warm up the voice well before any stressful event and stay in Second Circle voice to reach and touch your audience. When you are very nervous, use extra clarity of articulation to contain your vocal nerves and the related need to rush; slow down and stay meaning every word you speak as you speak it.

Lastly, fear can glaze your eyes over so look around you to see objects as clearly as possible. You can pause at any point of a presentation to breathe and look at the audience to harness your energy, as long as you don't freeze up in the pause but stay actively in your presence.

YOUR EGO

None of us have met a successful person or one that is working to be successful who doesn't have a healthy dollop of ego, but if your ego moves out of the healthy place into the vanity, superiority and arrogance of Third Circle, or gets battered into the 'I need to be liked' self-consciousness of First Circle, then you are facing another batch of enemies to your power presentations. An over- or under-inflated ego will knock you out of Second Circle and place an agenda on everything you say. The Third Circle agenda communicates, 'I'm better than you and I underestimate you.' In First Circle the communication agenda is the reverse: 'I shouldn't be here, please be nice to me and I overestimate you.'

Most of us work a lifetime on the negative effects of our egos so I cannot offer any quick fixes. However there are three points of focus I have found over years working with actors that can help, particularly if you are in Second Circle which, in its energy, is about a connection to others, not yourself.

1. Everyone wants to be liked but if you think about it rationally, you know it is something you can't control. The truth is, if you have 20 people in a room, somebody is likely not to like you and you can't do anything about it! I would suggest that the more you try to be liked, the worse it will be. Equally important, it is all right not to be liked by certain people. I would seriously worry if Hitler had liked me! All you can do is believe in your work and perform as best you can in any circumstance.

2. As soon as an actor believes they are better than the play or the audience then they are sliding into narcissism. The great actors have humility, insomuch as they

have a respect for their material and for the audience. I have heard many say that their job is to tell the story as written and that there is bound to be a member of the audience that knows more about their character's issues than they do. Everyone can apply those points of concentration into their work before and through a presentation.

3. You can prepare in Second Circle and you will feel when your ego interferes with your preparation. These interferences can be as simple as, 'I'll make them like me with this story', 'This will impress them', 'They won't understand this'. You get the picture. As these voices appear in your preparation you must work on staying in Second Circle and assess whether the 'voice' is valid and whether you need to change your ego or the material to stay fully direct and truthful.

The trouble with a Third Circle ego is that it can lead to you not fully understanding the threats around you. You can become oblivious to the plotters. A First Circle ego can infuriate those you work with because they believe you are withholding information when you are actually just worrying about yourself. It came as a mortifying shock to a CEO of a huge financial company that his board was plotting to overthrow him. He was so pleased with himself and preoccupied with his own ideas that he failed to notice how resentful his ego made all around him feel. A highly intelligent First Circle manager was equally shocked when she discovered that her self-preoccupation was seen as a devious technique to control those around her.

In both cases, egos had severed them from clearly perceiving their colleagues. Actually, as soon as they both began to work in Second Circle, they realized, in different ways, how much they were valued when ego-free.

COSMETIC
CONSIDERATIONS

You will want to look your best at meetings and presentations but there are important considerations and balances to get right, as not all the accessories we enjoy are useful if we want to present with our full power.

Power dressing has been a preoccupation for some time, although you must be careful that this cosmetic approach doesn't encase you in a wonderful-looking shell that blocks your true presence. Whatever you choose to wear for any event you must practise and work in the clothes and shoes and, most importantly, not allow anyone to interfere with what you are wearing immediately before an event. Don't ever wear something that puts you out of your comfort zone and is given to you without adequate rehearsal time.

Recently a brilliant financial spokesman came to me after watching himself on National Television. His presentation on TV looked like he was a wooden puppet. This was strange as he normally presented very effectively. It turns out that he allowed the interviewer, before he went on air, to suggest he pulled his jacket tightly over his chest to remove some crease mark. This spokesman was then so worried about his jacket that he didn't dare move. Another client was distressed that he had performed so badly as an after-dinner speaker at a City of London banquet. He was a very good speaker but had experienced a panic attack during his speech and, unable to continue, had to end it halfway through. It turned out that he had to wear very formal attire for the event which included a white tie and a cummerbund around his waist and, crucially, the abdominal area. He couldn't properly breathe or move his head and although he felt uncomfortable as he dressed, it hadn't occurred to him that he should rehearse in these clothes, which would have given him a chance to adjust them. That might have only meant loosening his collar and cummerbund a couple of inches.

Then there was the CEO of a TV company who was battling her chairman. Now it just so happened that her chairman was short and she decided at a crucial meeting to wear extra-high heels to intimidate him. Maybe that was a good tactic but not a good one to do without practice in those high heels. All that happened was she wobbled throughout her presentation and lost her breath and the power struggle.

Remember that clothes that impede your stance, body and breath will take you out of Second Circle. The crucial areas are your feet, which need to make that critical contact with the ground. Any clothes that weigh heavily on your shoulders or are tight around your neck, ribcage and stomach area will prove problematic to your presentation. If someone makes you up before a TV presentation, keep moving your face so it doesn't stiffen your muscles.

Hair is important, particularly if it is a fragile style or it is pulling your face taut – tight hair placement will pull facial muscles and can distort speech. Avoid hairstyles that hide your face and eyes. This is particularly important if you are speaking in a large room or space. Eyes communicate over space and hair will block this vital aid in engaging an audience. Watch out for jewellery that annoys your hands, neck or ears; this can include a chain of office, medals or even a tiara. The weight of the jewellery or its balance on your body can have a huge impact on your ability to stay present, connected and, there-fore, communicate.

The most efficient clothes are ones that you can feel physi-cally released in and breathe in. Shoes should enable you to feel the ground and stay solid on it. Wear any new clothes, shoes or accessories as you prepare for a presentation and adjust any tightness. Stand, sit and walk in the clothes. Move your shoulders and arms to feel any tension and adjust. Stretch in the clothes as much as possible and be prepared to abandon the outfit if you cannot move in it in Second Circle. In my youth, when I was a sales assistant in a major London store, I was intrigued watching a woman try on a series of skirts, leave the changing room wearing each skirt, sit down and open her knees. When she saw my intrigue, she said, 'I play the cello in an orchestra and must make sure I can wear skirts that allow me to play.' The lesson stuck with me. With your shoes, centre on the floor without shoes and then put the shoes on and adjust to find whether you can still feel the floor and how much adjustment you need to make throughout your body. Repeat this until you feel the shoes are manageable and that you can still stay in Second Circle with them on. The more extreme the heels, the more you have to practise being in them, as some shoes might have to be abandoned.

Always err on the side of Second Circle presence in your body and breath rather than cosmetic impact. Your message is more important than a look that impedes the content of your presentation. That is unless you are faced with having to distract an audience by your cosmetic appeal because you have nothing to say. A very glamorous politician once said to me, 'I only look really great when I have nothing to say.'

TECHNOLOGY

In my experience, many people fail miserably when they present with the aid of technology. I think there are two main reasons for this.

1. There is an assumption that the technology will do the work for you. That is because when you are amplified

and have visuals you feel the work will be done and that you don't have to work so hard or stay fully present.
2. People don't practise enough with technology within their rehearsal slots.

Using technology and presenting with it well is an extremely sophisticated skill which needs diligent work and repetition. Without the preparation, it is potentially disastrous.

I believe that presenting with technology takes more preparation than having none. That is, unless you are all show and no content. If you have good content you must stay fully present with the technology or it will swamp you.

Amplification

Many speakers rely too much on microphones and treat them as saviours. This results in a reduction in the voice, range, eye contact, breath and presence of the speaker. Amplification only amplifies what you produce, so if it reduces you, then this reduction is amplified to the audience. With any form of amplification, you still need to reach out to the audience in Second Circle, you need to breathe the space, allow the words to move the range of your voice, sustain a present energy through the presentation and articulate clearly the ends of words. Microphones actually require more precision in your technique. If you are gasping your breath, the audience will hear that gasp just as they will hear mumbling as louder mumbling, not clearer speech.

A body mike is clipped on to you near your throat and has a small pack placed behind you, usually on your waistband. This can pull you into First Circle if you are not consciously working through these physical restrictions. Present as though you were mike-free. You don't need extra vocal energy with amplification but all the Second Circle body, breath and voice needs to be still in place. Your head should not be tucked in to connect with the mike but still up so that you can connect with the audience.

The same applies to hand and standing microphones. Keep the hand mike steady and just below your mouth, being careful not to tuck your head down or tighten your shoulders. You must still look around at your audience and not glaze over. Be aware with a standing microphone not to tighten the whole body as you stay focused on one point. It is useful to stay released through your knees if standing, and to keep your feet on the floor with the energy on the balls of your feet. This applies to standing and sitting addressing a microphone. Keep breathing low and get eye contact with your audience. This simple technique really helps in radio interviews. One word of warning. When wearing a radio mike, be careful if you are wired and switched on before or after a presentation not to utter indiscretions. Your joke about the CEO might be communicated to the conference. One presenter in New York got a huge round of applause as he walked on before his speech. He had no idea why until he realized that the whole audience had heard every stage of his visit to the toilet before his entrance.

Visual Aids

Always remember you should be more interesting than charts or images on a screen or flip-chart. If that is not true then you are not needed in a presentation; a film would be better.

That sounds very harsh of me, but if you are using visual aids as a shield or as a quick fix instead of doing real preparation, then you must question whether you need to be there or not. When you present with aids your presence has to be heightened above and through the aids. For instance, don't look and speak in the direction of the aid, be it a chart or a screen. If you have to look, look and then turn out to the audience before speaking. In effect, you are staying present with the aid, taking energy from it and moving with that energy back to the audience. You are present with the aid but are always communicating in Second Circle with the audience. This proves to the audience that they are more important than a chart or an image.

As you prepare with visual aids be very critical as to how much you need them and how your presentation might have more impact without them. Remember that we are all so used to amazing images on film and TV. You are actually more potent than a pie chart and your humanity more moving than moving images. And remember that technology can fail so that your presentation should be able to work without it – it is merely an aid.

Telephone, Conference Calls and Video Links

The telephone can be a barrier to good communication. The main problem is that you relax too much into First Circle, particularly when someone else is speaking.

The old trick of standing up when taking a difficult phone call is a quick way of placing you into Second Circle.

Never relax out of Second Circle. Talk through the instruments with present energy and don't glaze over or get distracted or switch off when another party is talking. Listen in Second. Remember that we can all identify when someone we are talking to on the telephone is doing another task as we speak. If the call matters, then put all your energy into the call.

Autocues

Many speakers use autocues in crucial and large presentations. There are many occasions when a presentation has to be precisely scripted. Off by heart is obviously the most powerful form of presentation, followed by working off structured notes. However, sometimes the content cannot be learned in time or the material is so serious or potentially dangerous that it would be unwise not to use an autocue. With autocue, words move along a screen which is as close to your eyeline as possible, but is placed in such a way that you don't lose eye contact with your audience. The words move with you and that movement is controlled by a (hopefully) good technician.

If you spend a moment watching a good newsreader you will see how an autocue can be used. There are two non-negotiable skills required when using an autocue. The first is sight-reading.

All presenters should practise the skill of reading on sight. The development of good sight-reading is made easier when you are completely in Second Circle but still, the development of the skill demands a lot of repetition. The work is not complex – you need to glance at a reading and begin to read aloud, get your eyes off the book, make contact in Second Circle with your audience, which could be a camera, and then find your way back to the book without panic to gather the next series of words. As you repeat this task, your sight-reading will improve and you will learn to scan ahead to see where the thoughts and pauses are. You should practise this enough until you can make sense of what you are speaking. Practise this sight-reading from a book and work to get your eye contact out to a full audience so that the words are filling a theatre. Then repeat, imagining you are speaking to a camera. The next skill is to practise reading from a screen. You can reproduce this scenario by reading from a computer screen or by printing out a speech and pinning it on a wall. The aim of this practice is to sight-read and turn seamlessly to an audience in Second Circle to speak. When these skills are done well, the audience doesn't know that the autocue is there.

If you are going to use an autocue, you should have prepared your speech so that you use the autocue as a sophisticated and accurate reminder of your presentation. This allows you to give more than a clear sight-reading but an impassioned speech. Barack Obama often uses autocues. Observe his speeches carefully and you will realize that there is one on either side of the microphone. He knows the speeches, but he uses the autocue as a reminder. This enables him to get passionate in his addresses but stay on track. The only problem he initially had with the autocues was that his head went from side to side, going from one screen to the other and speaking to the placing of the screens, and rarely speaking out in front to the main body of the audience. Then he made the simple adjustment of taking words from one screen and looking out to the audience and speaking before going to the other screen and repeating the process.

Some presenters get so good with the autocue that they fall into the trap of traps. Never rely on the autocue to such an extent that you don't prepare a speech. There is a famous story about a wonderful presenter, a politician, who relied on his natural charisma and charm to beguile an audience. He never prepared any speech as he was brilliant with the autocue. He relied on a team of researchers and writers for his material and, actually, his authenticity. He depended on an autocue to feed him their material and never prepared or even bothered to find out who his audience was or what he was discussing at any particular meeting. He would switch on his charm, turn up at an event and read. After some years, his team were tired and angry at his cavalier and ungracious attitude to their work. So they all prepared and timed his downfall precisely. One day, he had a presentation that could change his world and actually the world of others.

He arrived, ever so slightly late, making an entrance. Finely dressed and coiffed, in beautiful natural voice. He walked on to the stage with all the confidence in the world but had not researched the subject of the presentation and did not know his audience. He started well, made the audience laugh and glanced at the autocue to make his first point. The autocue obliged and he started a seemingly knowledgeable presentation. Two thoughts into the presentation, he glanced up to get the next idea. On the autocue screen were six words.

'You are on your own now.'

Followed by a blank screen.

Of course, no charm or cosmetic skill in speaking could extract him from acute humiliation and a severe career blow.

Emails and Texts

The reason why so many emails and texts can appear rude and stark, if not brutal, is that they are not written in Second Circle! They are written in First or Third Circle language and often dashed out with very little care.

Quite simply, you have to imagine facing the receiver in person as you write an email or text. That doesn't mean you can't use shorthand but you should still have the receiver in mind as a human being. You must take particular care if it is a difficult message and you must apply all the techniques of Second Circle communication as you structure and write through technology. Use your imagination to flesh out the receiver and recognize how they might respond to the material.

The problem of rude emails and texts is such an issue in some workplaces that they have been banned when important or difficult information has to be communicated. The belief is that difficult communication should be done in person and that, in my terminology, means fully present in Second Circle. As my grandmother used to say, 'Treat as you would be treated.' Simple but humane advice, particularly when the object of communication is not present in the flesh.

Part 2

Power Presentation in Practice

1 Presentations

If you are presenting then it is a given that you have something important to say. You might even be in a position where you have to rally the troops.

Practice

I cannot tell you how many people arrive for coaching unprepared. When I ask them how they prepare I discover their practice has been silent and passive. This is not practice, as you cannot prepare to speak with presence without practising aloud your breath, voice or speech muscles. Power and energy are physical and you cannot do this in your head. Head learning is no good for your presence or confidence.

- Practise out loud. By that I do not mean mumbling or physically shuffling but fully and vigorously. Physically wrestle with your presentation.

- Get into your body.

- Breathe low and with full power engaging the support.

- Speak out in a focused Second Circle. Place the words into space.

- Articulate clearly every syllable.

When you practise in this way you will know whether you are achieving effective Second Circle communication. Until you fully commit to your voice and material you do not know what you have got and whether you can fulfil the task ahead of you.

Is the material yours? If it is, do you feel comfortable with the words or are you trying too hard or being too casual? The balance between formal and informal is crucial. If you are too formal you will offend and if you are too informal you will also offend. Make sure you are speaking words that you feel comfortable with and can own and imagine, but ones that won't offend. This balance is crucial if you are to sound authentic but not offensive. A misplaced joke can, in certain circumstances, destroy your career.

If the words are not yours, work on them so you can truthfully commit to them. You will need to connect to all the words and imagine them and their impact on the audience.

Research your audience. Never fail to know who your audience is. This can mean researching one person if the audience is one person. Again, this is a balancing act as you don't want to patronize, offend or go over their heads! All of these could happen, but a present concentration on your audience as you prepare will minimize the risk.

Practise the structures of your speech. What is the journey and story of the speech? Believe the story is important. If you don't have enough time to prepare fully, still get the basic structure of the story and journey you want the audience to make with you. When the structures are in place you will have a chance to change structure and make diversions, if the audience requires a change of focus.

Is there a rhythm to your presentation? Is there a pace? As you prepare you will begin to avoid embarrassing pauses, hesitation, random repetitions or non-verbal sounds that can only annoy and confuse the audience. You know that hums and ahs block the forward motion of presence and can only impede you and the audience.

Prepare sitting, standing and walking. This might mean

holding a microphone. In preparing, cover all possibilities, and that includes imagining the worst that can happen. Really! When I suggested this 'worst scenario' idea at a workshop it was met with some horror. One person said, 'I would never speak in public if I did that.' Well, I believe that you make yourself very vulnerable and stand very close to disaster if you don't imagine the worst happening in a presentation. In fact, many clients come to me because the worst did happen and they were so ill-prepared that they stood speechless and failed to recover. The scenarios I have met with clients include arriving to present and finding out the person you are going to criticize is in the audience, or not preparing for the Q & A session and being floored after a great presentation by an unimagined question. Prepare for a cynical member of the audience announcing before your presentation, 'Oh, you aren't going to discuss that idea are you?' And 'that idea' is the foundation of your presentation.

These are horror stories I hear all the time, but if you are prepared for them you will have a chance to deal with the horror. I came from theatre and actors do fall off the stage and have to get back on stage and continue. I have taught many stand-up comics and we have practised out loud all the worst possible heckles and prepared replies which are always delivered to the heckler in a full Second Circle energy.

Make a list – speak out the worst scenarios and the worst possible questions or interruptions you might face. By looking at these possibilities you prepare for them and they then are less likely to occur! This process always adds to the presentation and has actually given some of my clients new ideas. It can be very creative and liberating to face the horror.

Prepare

Prepare in Second Circle and realistically know how much time you have to prepare. You can't have too much time and the sooner you start preparing, the better. If it's only a day, make room in that day for preparation.

There are five points of preparation:

1. Content
2. Body, breath, voice and speech
3. Focus on the audience and what they need
4. Space, props and technology
5. Preparation immediately before the event.

1. Content

- How long is the presentation to be? Avoid going over time. Know the boundaries of time and always understand what and why you are communicating in the presentation.

- Write clear notes about your purpose and what you know and can offer the presentation.

- Trust your knowledge and be clear about the points you and only you can make.

- Stay present with yourself as you honour your unique contribution to your presentation.

- What is the story you wish to tell?

- What do you want to reveal?

- How can you educate the audience?

- Do you believe your content enough to be passionate? If not, try to find passion within the content.

- Structure your presentation with a beginning, middle and ending. How will you begin? Try to be direct and exciting. Open up the story. Then work to take the audience on a journey forward towards a conclusion. As you prepare, imagine that the conclusion could transform the audience's thinking.

- The most important thing you can do is speak the whole presentation out loud.

- Practise your thoughts and speak them in Second Circle with energy and direction.

- This process can take time but keep doing it until you feel a strong form in your content.

- At this point, write down the structure and content of your presentation.

Many people fail with the content of a presentation because they try a style of presentation they are not happy with and know they can't really do. Recently an executive I was working with said to me, 'My boss tells me I should tell a few jokes to make the audience laugh but I can't tell jokes.' Don't do what you know you can't do. What works for others won't necessarily work for you. If my suggested styles make you uncomfortable, don't risk feeling that way. A female client had a lovely sense of humour which she began to work into her content. She didn't tell jokes but she does now make audiences laugh with her own style of language.

It is at this moment that you must start to make a decision about whether you present from notes, learn the whole presentation by heart, or just read it. Play with these three options and as long as you have time you don't need to decide how you will present until nearer the event. Most people who are frightened of presenting need to have some form of notes as a safety net but I'll address this option later.

2. Body, Breath, Voice and Speech

- Even as you begin to know your content, start preparing it with the body, breath, voice and speech actively and aloud, avoiding preparing slumped in an armchair, at a desk or mumbling.

- Stand or sit ready and actively in Second Circle.

- Speak whatever content you have in this position.

- Breathe and support with the breath the content as it develops in your head and heart.

- Fully voice the content. Even intone it to a Second Circle point and then speak it.

- Fully articulate the words. The act of physical and vocal commitment in the early stages of preparation will actually help you to develop and hone the content. Fully expressing an idea will quickly tell you whether it works or doesn't work.

- Please don't be afraid of changing the content as you work. Generally, if you sense you should change something, that instinct is normally accurate.

- After each exercise, write relevant notes. What works, what doesn't work? Do I need more articulation? Do I need more breath, etc?

By this stage your presentation will be taking palpable form and shape. It will have started to be alive and vital.

3. Focus on the Audience and What They Need

- Spend time imagining the audience and researching them. What do they expect and need, even if that knowledge will be hard to hear?

- What are you trying to achieve with the audience?

- Are you there to inform and educate them?

- Or are you there to praise and thank them?

- Is your intention to inspire and take them all to new heights?

- Contemplate the above in Second Circle and you will probably discover that you need to do all three.

- Be clear as to your strengths and put those strengths into your content.

- Be equally clear about your weaknesses and then try to find ideas and stories that will help you cope with your weaknesses.

- Praise, challenge and inform with truth.

Assess whether the audience will be on your side or whether they will be bored by your subject or even antagonistic. This will be difficult but it is better to imagine all possibilities rather than keep your head in the sand! It is always easy to ignore the hard issues in a First or Third Circle attitude. In Second Circle you have a chance to face the truth, which can only make you stronger.

4. Space, Props and Technology

This section is about research. You might already know the space you will be presenting in but if you don't know it, find out as much as you can about all the details in and around the space.

- How big is the space?

- How many people will be there?

- Am I on a stage above the audience or are they sloping up from me?

- Are the audience in front of me or are they on three sides of me?

- Do I walk out in front of them from a wing or do I have to climb stairs to get to the place of presentation?

- Do I sit in view of the audience before presenting?

- Is the stage carpeted or wood?

- Is it raked – that is, is it sloped?

- Am I standing behind a lectern or standing alone?

- How am I lit? If so, can I see the audience?

- Will I be miked and if so how? Is it a standing mike, one that is fixed to me, or a hand mike?

- What type of miking would you prefer and is that preference possible?

- If you are using visual aids, find out if you have to operate them, and if not, who is?

- Make sure there is room-temperature water within easy reach.

- Find out what the audience has just done. After lunch is harder, as is around 4.00pm as their attention span is harder to access.

Even if you can get answers to half these questions, you will be better prepared than most, and you have started to imagine yourself in the space, which actually helps diminish fear.

You will begin to recognize the demands required of the presentation. For instance, you will begin to know how much breath you will need to practise with; whether the lighting situation allows Second Circle eye contact with the audience; whether you are behind a lectern that can support your notes or whether you have to hold them. If there is a choice, take the situation that helps you stay present. Choose the amplification you prefer or if there is not a choice, start preparing with the miking you will have to use. Your research will tell you what sort of entrance you have to make – up steps or out across a large platform. This can then be practised in Second Circle.

Find out what sort of clothes would be suitable for the event and start to work in clothes that are acceptable but also comfortable for you. Shoes that help you contact the floor are essential, especially if you are presenting on a rake or carpet.

If you know the space that you are about to present in you still need to think carefully about the space and think it through from your perspective. It would be most useful to go and hear someone else present in the space and be very attentive to all the above questions, as they perform.

Let me be honest, presenting is dangerous and difficult and things do go wrong. The research might seem pointless but this is the point. The more you know and imagine about an event, the more chance you have to negotiate the problems and therefore succeed.

Great presenters take nothing for granted and by covering all possible bases they can trust their content and delivery more and more. They have a chance to be in Second Circle. Believe me when I say that the more you do this basic research, the more enjoyment you will get in presenting. Very quickly these research questions will become organic to you and your assessment of every space and event, rapid and accurate. In other words, you will start to become a professional speaker, not an amateur one. In theatre we have a saying: 'Amateur actors believe it will be all right on the night, professional ones know it won't.' They prepare.

5. Preparation Immediately Before the Event

The day before you present, speak the whole presentation aloud and with full Second Circle energy.

- If you make mistakes, don't worry and don't stop as it is important to feel the required energy and length of the piece.

- Use whatever props you are going to use and wear the appropriate clothing.

On the day, give yourself time at the venue. Don't risk being late as that will increase your fear a hundred-fold.

- If it is possible to get into the venue on your own beforehand, grab this opportunity.

- Practise walking on stage in Second Circle or up the steps, etc.

- Stand centre stage and breathe the space until you feel your breath touches all around the auditorium. Do this very calmly.

- Stand by the lectern or where you know you will have to stand.

- Speak out into the space without any amplification, just to sound your voice in the space.

- If you are using notes, where are they going to be put? Where is the water?

- Go and sit in one of the furthest seats in the space to see how the space looks from there. Generally you will be surprised to realize how small you look from the audience's point of view and therefore how present you need to be.

- Lastly, go and stand where you will make your entrance and breathe. Search out a solid wall nearby in case you need to push it to contact your breath before your entrance. If you are sitting in view before starting you can feel the floor through the balls of your feet and push down on an armrest.

You must eat before an important presentation, but make it a light meal an hour or so before.

Try to give yourself a five-to-ten-minute period of time alone and without distractions.

- Check your body and release any tensions in your shoulders, jaw, upper chest, spine or knees.

- Warm up your breath: a few deep breaths pushing against a wall or the flopping-over hug to open the back of your ribcage.

- Gently hum to warm up your voice and move into an 'ooh' to a point to place the voice into Second Circle.

- Warm up your articulation and practise the first thought of your presentation.

- Sit quietly and focus your mind on what you need to tell the audience, the story of your presentation.

As you wait to go on, breathe low through your fear and keep the shoulders released.

- Keep breathing as you go on and as you stand, breathe the space and look around it, making real Second Circle eye contact.

- Start on the breath.

- If you make a mistake, it doesn't matter. Cancel and continue. Everyone makes mistakes, keep on going, people won't notice. They will notice if you comment on the mistake because you will have come out of Second Circle.

- Trust your material and be passionate if you feel passionate.

- Stay present and the audience will come along with you.

- Energy is contagious. If you feel they are in First or Third Circle, don't be led into their energy. Stay present. If you are habitually Third Circle you might be tempted to overrally a First Circle audience or face off with a Third Circle one. If your habit is First Circle, any non-present audience will encourage you back into First Circle. Fight these temptations and stay present.

It is possible that you have to make a presentation with only a day's notice. If that is the case then you need to work all these points rapidly and yet efficiently. The best scenario is that you have a few weeks' notice or that you give yourself at least two weeks' preparation time.

When you have done enough preparation you will begin to realize that you can learn your presentation by heart and, even better, realize that as you get skilled at this craft you can know your structures and speak to your audience in the moment without a word-for-word planned text.

This is the sign of a really great speaker.

Meeting the Challenges of Space

Your energy has to match any space you work in so that means your body, breath and voice have to reach out to the perimeters of any space you are presenting in.

We all know that a larger space will take work but a possible trap when presenting in small spaces is that they can beguile you into a false sense of security. You can become too casual, so much so that you become inaudible. Interestingly, an audience might forgive you for being inaudible in a huge space but they will be unforgiving if you are inaudible in a space smaller than an average living room.

Let us look at the challenges of space and how you can work in different spaces. You know whether you prefer intimate presentations to large ones so ask yourself: do I like the large spaces because I can push energy out and not really connect to the audience but control them? Do I prefer small venues because I can stay in my shell and not really reveal or share anything of myself? You now realize a 'yes' answer to either question is not viable if you want to present with power.

How To Stay Present To and In Every Space

If you have an important meeting or presentation, try to visit the space beforehand and even if you know the space, go to it again and check the dynamics and acoustics.

What kind of acoustics does the space have? To check this

you have to find out whether the space is live or dead. A live acoustic has an echo and will require more diction. If you speak in the space and it is live you will feel your voice echo back on you. If you cannot hear any response to your voice as you speak, you are in a dead space and your voice is being absorbed into the fabric of the space. These spaces will require more resonance to penetrate through to the audience. The audience also absorbs sound so a large audience will have the effect of deadening your voice. This means a live empty space will improve with an audience, a dead empty space will get more dead with bodies in it.

What materials are there in the room? Carpets, curtains and drapes can smother the voice; concrete sharpens it; wood and plaster are wonderful for the projection of the human voice and those spaces have been designed for the maximum aid in live communication.

- When alone in the space, place yourself where you will present from and breathe the space. Imagine your breath going to every corner of the room.

- Release your voice on an 'ooh' into a 'ha' to touch the space with sound and be most aware of not falling off the sound into First Circle voice. Stay in Second Circle until the end of the sound and finish it without any fall.

- Count over ten by building up the numbers and sustaining the counts in the space: 1, breathe, 12, 123, etc. Feel each release move out through the space and direct your voice through the counts to specific seats, staying in contact with the whole space throughout your body and breath.

- If you know how you will begin your presentation, practise the beginning in the space. Intone a few words and then speak them without pushing.

- Remember that big spaces require more diction so practise with speaking ends of words and defining multisyllabic words.

- End by staying very still and knowing that the space is yours as you enter and present and that what you have to say is important and you need to communicate your material to the audience.

I realize that visiting a space is a luxury so here is how to cope when you enter an unknown space where you haven't had the opportunity to practise.

- Enter in Second Circle body, with physical pace and clarity.

- Before entering, if there is an opportunity to push against a wall to engage the lower breath, take that opportunity. Even one hand on a door frame will be of enormous use.

- As you enter the space, look around and breathe it and as you do so, make eye contact with your audience.

- Really take time to feel the breath and the readiness of your support in the lower abdominal area before you start speaking.

- Reach out to the audience in Second Circle by staying on the balls of your feet. Stay on your voice and be sure you articulate. Check in with the audience to make sure you are really meeting them with your presence and don't give up that presence if they are in First or Third Circle.

- Take into account the height of the space and how that affects your body.

- In a small space, stay present throughout your body, don't allow the space or number of people to squash you. This means you have to fight the desire to go casual and reduce yourself into First Circle.

- In a large space, avoid pushing your body and voice into Third Circle or fidgeting and giving your energy away into First Circle.

When you have to wait for a period of time before speaking do stay present; this is particularly important if the audience can see you. Your nerves or impatience can be observed by all. And please don't let people interfere with your concentration as you prepare and want to stay present. This attention could be well meant but can fuss you out of your energy. You need to ask politely to be left alone and please don't feel that you have to entertain others before an important event. You must conserve your energy.

Be aware that audience energy is contagious to you, so if fifty people are bored before you begin a presentation, it is easy for you to retreat into First or battle out into Third Circle. Stay present and connected. In a small meeting and space, this contagious energy can be more potent and your negative reactions more destructive to you.

Remember not to relax your positive energy when you turn your back on the audience or as you leave the space.

You will soon know the spaces that make you more comfortable, but you still have to work to feel the same ease in the less comfortable ones. You can practise by imagining the hard spaces and working through your physical reactions to them to conquer those arenas.

The Group and Intimacy

Some people are better at presenting to large groups and others are better in more intimate surroundings.

This section will help you marry those skills and make you realize that a great presenter can do both.

The scale of a group is unimportant if you are connected through your body, breath, voice, mind and heart in Second Circle, so if you have a preference in size of group, it is because you are using scale to hide your presence rather than reveal it.

Large groups do take more energy from you. You have to expand yourself but not into an overblown Third Circle. If you do this you might feel more comfortable and protected than when you are more exposed in an intimate setting. However, if you can connect to a large group in Second Circle, you can equally connect in Second Circle in more intimate scenarios.

Small Groups

If a large group is comfortable in Second Circle, all you need to do is transfer that energy into a smaller space.

Try this as an exercise.

- Go into a big space; a large room will do the job.

- Take a Second Circle physical stance and breathe the space until you feel connected to it.

- Now speak in the space until you feel you are filling it with Second Circle vocal energy. Avoid pushing or allowing your voice to fall back into First Circle.

- When you feel connected in the space go and sit in a chair with another chair opposite you. Stay in Second

Circle and now breathe to the chair until you feel your breath has reduced from the big space but is still active and dynamic and touching the chair.

- At this point, speak the words more intimately to the chair and an imagined person.

- What you should be feeling is a diminishing tension but one that still keeps you in Second Circle, not reducing into First Circle.

By going out into the space you appreciate the focus of the work and then with the same Second Circle tension, you are able to reduce that focus to an intimate setting.

You might need to repeat this re-placing of energy but eventually you will understand you can be as intimate and effective in a small space as you are in a larger one.

Large Groups

Now let us examine the reverse use of energy.

This exercise is for the people who know they are more effective in Second Circle in an intimate setting.

- Find a large space – it can be a large room but it is important that the large size of the room makes you feel uncomfortable.

- Set the space up in this way: Place two chairs opposite one another so that you can construct a space that you are normally comfortable in.

- Sit down in the chair that faces out in the space but concentrate on the chair opposite you.

- Sit in Second Circle, alert and present.

- Breathe to the opposite chair and then speak a few sentences to that chair in Second Circle. Do so until you feel fully connected and reaching that chair.

- This should be easy as this is where you excel.

- When this connection feels secure, shift your focus to a point beyond the chair in the space and imagine the person you are speaking to is further away.

- Breathe to them, speak to them until you feel connected across that new distance with the person.

- At that point, shift the imagined person further away and repeat, speaking with Second Circle breath and voice until you feel connected.

- Do this shift of distance until the imagined person is at the back of the room.

- When you feel a connection across this distance, expand your focus to include the sweep of the whole room.

- You are now taking the quality of your Second Circle intimate connection to the whole space.

As you do this exercise and succeed in it, perform the same process in larger spaces until you physically and organically understand how your intimate work can extend out into ever larger groups of people.

Question and Answer Sessions

By now you realize that I believe you should always contemplate the worst scenarios in a sensible Second Circle way.

So many great presentations fail in the Question and Answer session. What tends to happen is that after a great presentation, you can relax too much into First or enter a place of self-congratulation and move into Third Circle. Both shifts can make you open to a difficult question from the audience.

This Q & A vulnerability is equally possible in smaller meetings if you aren't sufficiently prepared.

Dealing with Q & As

Here are the points you have to consider:

- Practise aloud and in Second Circle all the possible difficult questions and then practise the answers.

- After finishing a presentation, don't take anything for granted, relax, or feel too pleased with yourself.

- When you get a difficult question, breathe and stay centred, look in Second Circle to the questioner, breathe to them and answer them carefully and with due respect.

- If someone wants to rattle you, they want you to move either into First or Third Circle. The very act of acknowledging them in Second Circle will give them a sense of relief and respect.

- If you answer them in Second Circle and they still want to make trouble then you still have to finish the debate with them in Second Circle.

My experience informs me that most difficult questioners are silenced by Second Circle focus on them and a clear Second Circle reply. The rage of a questioner is fuelled by a presenter treating them in an off-hand, First Circle manner or a Third Circle attack.

Off the Cuff

All of the information in the Q & A section applies to off-the-cuff moments in presentations and meetings.

Off-the-cuff remarks are only a shock because they are not expected.

Expect them.

For instance, if you are at a meeting, you have to expect to be asked your opinion. Don't believe the meeting won't require you to give an opinion.

So during a presentation or a meeting, be actively aware of your responses and ideas as they occur to you and make notes if an idea settles on you.

I am not suggesting that you speak anything you don't feel is required, but by having a constant awareness of your ideas flowing through you, there will be a strong possibility that you can respond with clarity when challenged or asked for your opinion. If you think you are unimportant and won't be asked to contribute, you are in First Circle and eventually will be asked. A passive person at a meeting begins to annoy the ones who do contribute. A Third Circle over-contributor eventually riles others and an appropriate remark or idea gets ignored as an act of revenge. Be prepared to contribute, but always appropriately.

Reading Material

When you watch the news on TV or listen to the radio, you will often see or hear someone reading a statement badly. This is a disconnecting experience for the reader and for the audience.

Many people still cling to the idea that reading is safer than speaking to the world.

I understand that people in precarious circumstances cannot risk making the mistake of speaking a slanderous sentence so reading is a safe option, but you must realize that reading well is harder than speaking well.

This could be because the material is not yours, or you may have written it in a literary way rather than an oral one.

It is a frightening fact that you might be asked to read without any preparation and then you have to trust your sight-reading skills, which I have explored in the autocue section on page 158. Practise reading at sight but also practise any reading you know you have to do. Never believe it will be easy. When you have the luxury of preparation, read aloud with full Second Circle attention and then explore the reading with all the connection exercises of structure and ownership we have practised.

Prepare to work any reading at least three times before speaking it. When given a reading without any preparation time, go somewhere private – a toilet can be good – and mouth the reading, making sure you are breathing. This can be done in a few minutes but will save you.

Notes

Notes are clung to as a safety net, but they can give you a false sense of security.

You mustn't cling to the notes too tensely, pulling yourself into First Circle. You might believe that by writing out notes you don't have to prepare more fully. This is potentially disastrous. Notes work if you prepare fully and then write bullet points down that form your notes. Your notes are then a guide to you but not a saviour.

In this way, you will take the notes into a presentation or meeting as a safety net, and then not use them.

If you do need to check on your notes, you should stay in Second Circle with the audience as you look at the notes, breathe and read what you need to read, then seamlessly return to your audience.

Do not hide the fact that you have needed to look at your notes. In this way notes are part of your work process; you have not panicked but are still connected to your content and your audience.

Ten Steps to a Power Presentation

1. Give your presentation structure – a journey that moves forward from a strong start and seeks a conclusion through exploration. Prune any random words or ideas.
2. Practise out loud – focus on every word and idea at this point, so practise slowly and then build up to a natural speed. Then for the actual presentation you will need only a few short bullets to hand to keep you on track in case your presentation wanders.
3. Release your body tensions and warm up your voice.
4. Walk into the space with presence and natural confidence (not arrogance) and make eye contact with your audience.
5. Breathe to your audience so that you connect with them (don't breathe halfway to them, nor beyond or above them).
6. Stand centred and don't lock your knees.
7. If standing behind a lectern don't focus on the mike – you will become rigid and your energy stifled.
8. If holding a mike don't focus on speaking into it but out to the audience. Practice will make this easier.
9. Prepare for all the things that can go wrong!
10. Be yourself and believe in what you're saying.

Attending a Presentation

As you attend any presentation, there are two main pulls on your energy.

If the presenter is in Second Circle then you have an easy task and can stay in Second Circle with ease. You could find yourself in an audience of a First Circle bored brigade or a Third Circle challenging regiment. More likely there is a mixture of both and you have to fight the energy of the group to stay in Second Circle. If you don't fight to stay there you could miss a brilliant presentation.

If the speaker is in First then the whole audience will probably follow this energy and in this scenario you have to assess whether it suits the speaker to have you in First Circle and passive and malleable!

If the speaker is in a controlling Third Circle, you and the audience might feel repressed and sit back and take the manipulation, or you might be tempted to be hoisted up into a challenging Third.

Stay in Second Circle and begin to know the audience around you and the real skills and intentions of the presenter. In Second Circle you will not miss the important messages of the presentation and you will be more acutely aware of any lies in the content.

Presenting to the Media

The most prevalent energy you will probably face as you meet the media is a very casual First Circle. This approach has three probable reasons.

1. The television and radio crew and presenters are so used to turning out shows that they don't live the

excitement of media but stay on the borderline of boredom.

2. They are aware you are nervous broadcasting to thousands of people and believe that you must be calmed by their indifference.

3. More alarming for you, they are playing at being casual so that you take your guard down and they can then slaughter you on air in the interview.

There are great and caring media presenters and journalists but there are some who realize that destroying you as their interviewee will be a career boost and a bigger coup than placing you in a fair and good light. The worst aspect of the media is its love of disaster and exposure.

So be on guard and in Second Circle survival mode.

Prepare all possible questions, attacks or ingratiating remarks that can make you look vain.

Here are the questions you must ask yourself in full Second Circle presence:

- Why are you being interviewed?

- What do you know that the wider world should know?

- What do the media want from the interview?

- What do you need from the interview?

- What are the strengths of your knowledge?

- What are the weaknesses?

- What do you want to reveal?

- What do they want you to reveal?

- What are you not prepared to reveal?

- Is there going to be an attack, if so, where might it come and how can you defend yourself?

Even actively asking these questions will give your whole interview a firmer foundation.

Prepare

- Prepare aloud your opening statement but also be prepared for the interviewer to scupper that focus.

- Prepare what you are ready to speak about as opposed to the things you cannot speak about. Consequently, prepare to avoid, with as much clarity as you can, the unapproachable subjects.

- Prepare to lead the interview knowing that they might try to lead you but they could vainly show off their wit and knowledge instead of fully interviewing you.

- Before the interview, warm up and get into your body with your breath down.

- If you have the chance, check on the location of your interview and most importantly whether you are going to sit in a chair that allows you to be present with your feet on the ground and your breath low. Sofas and high stools can effortlessly take you out of Second Circle.

- During the interview, stay in Second Circle and breathe to the interviewer. Stay connected to them and listen attentively.

- If the questions are good, answer them, but if they are trivial, answer and steer the subject matter the way you want it to go!

- Maintain eye contact even if you are in a radio studio, stay present with the interviewer even during the commercial breaks. Don't lose focus or concentration as they shuffle their notes.

- On television, breathe to the interviewer and the camera. This double focus is hard but still possible in Second Circle. You can practise this with two points of focus before the interview.

- Avoid anger, cynicism and mocking; all these qualities will make you look and sound weak and deeply unattractive.

- Don't let flattery take you off your guard. Accept compliments with grace but don't be so satisfied that you retreat into First or preen yourself into Third Circle. If this happens you could have been set up and might get a question that penetrates your presence.

- Laugh at yourself but don't let this pull into self-mockery as you will then lose all your credence.

- Don't slander others or allow yourself to be ungracious about opponents.

- When you sense the interview is coming to a close, make sure you speak your final thoughts succinctly.

- Be aware that you might be asked to read material in the interview. This might be important if you have to make legal or careful statements but remember that reading is not easier than speaking.

- If a reading is given to you just before a broadcast, insist on reading it aloud at least three times before you have to read it on a live show.

- Be aware of the props you might encounter.

- On television you will probably be made up and that can immobilize your face.

- You will have a microphone pack on your body and a microphone attached to your upper chest. Don't allow these things to restrict your body or breath.

- As you sit down, you or your clothes might be placed in a restricting position. Free yourself as much as you can and make sure you can breathe and keep your shoulders released.

- The lights will be hot and that might upset you.

- Keep breathing as the interview gets close, don't go into a frozen state of fear and expectancy.

- On radio, breathe to the microphone but look at your interviewer.

- Speak to the interviewer, don't push yourself into an unattractive and insensitive Third or mumble in First Circle.

- A journalist will probably tape you and because there is no immediate pressure on you, you could relax too much and reveal on tape things that you should not reveal. Stay alert.

Watch, listen or read the interviews back and do so with a clear Second Circle alertness. Don't be so critical you miss the excellent parts of your presentation, or so pleased with yourself that you miss the negative moments.

Like everything else in life, these media encounters take practice and the more you do, the better you become as long as you stay in Second Circle.

2 Meetings

First Impressions

The first impression is crucial. The tools and craft you now have must be used from the first moment you appear in front of an audience, a single influential person, or any of your work team. Your human energy affects everyone around you and that includes the person who cleans your office. Even when you know who you are about to meet, treat that meeting as a first meeting and that mindset will centre you and show those you are meeting an energy of care and respect.

Always walk into any room with Second Circle energy. This might mean you have to walk with purpose down corridors before you reach the room or pace in your office before leaving. This will give your entrance and you immediate power, and impact positively on the meeting. When you are stressed or fearful before a first impression, push against a wall to engage your breath and body and as you come away from the wall, keep breathing, then move off with that energy into the room or on to the platform to present.

As you enter any space keep breathing calmly and as low in the body as you can. Breathe the space. Breathe to the individual or to the audience you are meeting. Aim to get eye contact with them. Don't force the contact or give way to their reluctance to meet your eyes. Stay connected. Seek eye contact with your whole body and breath and you will be present and unforgettable. You will also draw them to you and their positive energy out of them. Looking at someone with presence is recognizing who they are. You will not only impact on them but discover their authenticity! You might have to practise entering a room in Second Circle again and again. Do so when no-one is around, but do practise! The more you do it the more natural it becomes. There is a simple reason why performers make an impact as they enter a space. They practise entrances and exits for hundreds of hours.

When you are thinking in a meeting or presentation, let your mind think outwards rather than become too introspective. Use the energy of the space and those around you to gather your thoughts.

Sitting Into Standing

Greet those entering your territory with positive energy and focus. Practise standing up in Second Circle with a centred body and a full breath to the imagined person.

If you are the more powerful person, show generosity when you stand with presence to greet your visitor. Your energy will be contagious, or might expose any lack of generosity in the person you are greeting. Any First Circle dithering or Third Circle bravado will be challenged by your clear presence. I have encouraged many of the most powerful people on the planet to work on sitting into standing with full presence, breath and grace. Don't be ashamed of repetition, every great craftsperson in the world repeats and repeats.

If you are the inferior party in this meeting, you are probably waiting to be interviewed or invited into a space. While you are sitting awaiting the inevitable, do not relax into First Circle or pump yourself into Third Circle but stay present in your body and breath. Keep breathing as fluidly and as low as you can. Practise all this before the event and practise standing up with energy and presence in your body, breath and eye contact. Be very aware in the waiting area of the chair you are sitting in as it might be one of those cushy sofas that pull you back; if you are not aware of this you could find yourself fighting to get up. Perch yourself forward so that you are ready to stand easily and able to breathe naturally.

The Second Circle Leader

If you are the most powerful person at the meeting, your conduct in Second Circle will be most welcome and appreciated. You are treating those you meet as equals and this will instil good working relationships. We all long for leaders who know and use their power well and this knowledge is noticed on the First Meeting.

If a leader meets us in First Circle we have two clear impressions:

1. They do not know how to use power and could be weak.
2. They are hiding their power and are consequently going to use it when we least expect it and are potentially dangerous.

If a leader meets us in Third Circle – and this appears to be the most common problem – we feel inferior. The leader is signalling their superiority. We feel unneeded, unknown and irrelevant. We are possibly meeting a bully and we either shrink away or go into Third Circle for a potential face-off.

No-one wants to work for a Third Circle leader and it is even worse if we are treated in Third Circle while others are greeted in Second Circle. One of the key issues of a leader is to be consistent and fair and this is communicated in constant Second-Circle connection from a leader.

A leader can and should use power, and that will be respected if it is done in Second Circle.

Perhaps you are the perceived lowest status in the meeting

but it is equally important you stay in Second Circle as you meet people. In this way you keep your dignity and communicate who you are and that you are not a pushover (First Circle) or will have to be dealt with (Third Circle).

Actually, no-one wants to meet or ultimately work with either First Circle energy (who are they, what are they hiding, and will they contribute?) or Third Circle energy (do they think they are better than me, why are they controlling me or are they duping me, will they listen?).

- Whatever energy is thrown at you or denied, stay in Second Circle.

- Check your stance, your breath, breathe to whoever is producing negative energy. Maintain eye contact and continually speak to people.

- Do not concede. Stay present.

Shaking Hands on Meeting

We have all received the clammy handshake or the squeeze of an overly rigorous grip. Or the weak pat on the arm or back, or the slap that can range from mildly intrusive to quite painful! The same applies to hugs and kisses: the wimpy hug, the bear hug, the air kissing and the intrusive, overly sexual kiss. Greetings that are done with the wrong energy can make us feel unrecognized and irrelevant, or controlled and manipulated.

In a good, equal and generous greeting, move towards whoever you are greeting in Second Circle through your body, breath and eye contact. Connect with that person as you shake hands and introduce yourself with a confident, natural voice. As you finish the greeting, even if you are retreating physically, stay present with them.

Be aware of your physical distance from people. Take your space but don't invade other people's territory. Actually, the more you maintain Second Circle, the more you will naturally gauge the appropriate space between you and others around you.

Remember that energy is contagious so stay present even if others are not. This will make you memorable and unassailable. You will represent power on first acquaintance and that power will have a chance to be with you throughout the meeting or event. When you start well, you have much more chance of continuing well.

Leaving or Parting

Many a great meeting or presentation is sabotaged by the leaving or parting. The hesitation, the shrinking back, all create a lack of ending in parting that can undermine the success of a whole event or meeting.

Something is wrong if you are in charge of a meeting or event and people don't know that it has ended. We all need clear beginnings and endings. They are only accomplished by the leader being in Second Circle. Your parting is the final remembrance you leave with the client or audience. Go fully and with presence when you have to go. Don't dawdle and don't strut but be clear and defined.

Remember that the meeting is over when you are out of sight and gone. That means you have to stay present in the long walk across a large room or down a corridor as your presence is felt until you are no longer with the person or persons. Be defined as you leave and as you shake hands and say goodbye. Breathe, make eye contact. Don't linger in First Circle or control in Third Circle. Walk with presence and energy until you know no-one can see you.

Blueprint For a Successful Meeting

Conducting a meeting is complex but there are some very effective basic guidelines you can keep in mind.

Ten Questions to Ask Yourself Before a Meeting

1. Why am I conducting this meeting?
2. What do I want to achieve?
3. Am I prepared to change my opinions? If not, why am I conducting a meeting?
4. Who will be at the meeting and what are their roles?
5. What is my role?
6. Do I want certain people there? If not, why are they there?
7. Who am I prepared to listen to and who don't I trust?
8. If I don't trust them, what can I do about it?
9. What would be the best result of the meeting and what would be the worst result?
10. What time constraints are on the meeting?

I guarantee that if you speak out these questions with full Second Circle body, breath and voice and then write down, still in Second Circle, any answers, then you will begin to conduct meetings in Second Circle with great skill, humanity and knowledge.

The more dangerous and important the meeting, the more you should prepare in this way.

Attending a meeting probably means you are in a lower status role, so speak out the same questions with attendance in mind. Reinforce what you know and why you are there.

Leading a Meeting

It is a leader's job to actively move on the meeting, extract relevant information, recognize problems, solve problems or acknowledge that they cannot yet be solved, not waste time on repetition, but be efficient.

Listen well and constantly move the discussion forward and yet be open to new and relevant ideas.

All the above is only possible in Second Circle.

Start the meeting in Second Circle and look around to see who is present with you. Contact those in First or Third in Second Circle either through your energy or actually by saying something to them.

Start clearly and directly and reveal what you need from the meeting. Have in your mind the structure, that is of opening up a debate and exploring all relevant sections of the debate and then resolving and concluding some if not all of the questions raised.

Listen in Second Circle and seek information from those you know have knowledge, but don't be surprised if others have good ideas.

Control repetition and those who are speaking without knowledge.

It is easier to draw out a First Circle person than to stop a Third Circle person. Draw out First Circle by asking them clear questions about what they know. First Circle thinking tends to express only fragments of knowledge so you might have to probe for relevant knowledge. It is likely you will have to encourage a process that moves towards conclusions with questions like, 'Where do you think this idea will take us?' Be patient but not to the extent that the First Circle person can control the meeting through passive resistance or calculated withholding.

A Third Circle person can be harder to focus and you will be more tempted to move into Third Circle with them, particularly if they are annoying you. Stay very clearly in Second Circle with them. Third Circle thinking tends to pronounce conclusions without explaining how they got to them. They also can drive that conclusion home relentlessly, reinforcing it with personal anecdotes. It can help to ask them to explain the journey of their thoughts and ask them to think about other people's points of view. Well-educated Third Circle people can hide behind their education and need to be asked to express ideas simply and in pragmatic terms.

The leader should encourage each person in the meeting to speak to each other in Second Circle. Your example will help and gradually become positively contagious. The most obvious signs of people in Second is that they are sitting up, not slouched in their chairs, and not fidgeting with papers or doodling.

If you can control the environment, make sure the chairs aren't too comfortable, that there is good air and natural light, that the room is not too hot and that the room has minimum distractions. The clearer the space, the clearer the energy in the space.

You are a good leader if you can listen to everyone equally but also move the meeting forward away from repetition, subjects that cannot be dealt with in the meeting, personal attacks, trivia and past examples that have no present meaning.

Everyone attending should feel safe enough to express an opinion as long as it is relevant to the meeting.

By all means use and allow humour and personal stories if they still move the meeting forward and don't mock or hurt anyone present. As soon as this happens, you will have lost trust and the chance of creative thinking.

Attending a Meeting

The degrees of difficulty in staying in Second Circle when attending a meeting will entirely depend on whether the leader is present in Second Circle.

A First Circle leader is probably feeling safe or bored and if you can stay in Second Circle with them you have a real opportunity to shift them into their presence. If they are always in First Circle they are used to people either being bored around them or trying to topple them with the Third Circle bluff. Be interested in them in Second and you might open them up.

There is no guarantee that they will notice you if they stay in First Circle, locked away from you and the world, but others will be relieved that you bring into the room a clear, unthreatening energy.

A Third Circle leader will be operating in this energy to control and defeat opposition. Most people around them will be in First Circle apart from those who wish to have a confrontation.

Staying in Second Circle might confuse them but you will be noticed without the usual Third Circle threat. You might even bring them into Second Circle when you make clear enough points. This is a sign that they appreciate you and even see you as an equal.

If you are with a Second Circle leader it is essential, and much easier, to stay in Second Circle with them. They will definitely notice if you drift off into First or shield yourself in Third. Don't risk being inattentive with a Second Circle leader, as you will be discovered.

You can positively change your career by staying in Second Circle with a Second Circle leader. They will see in you a present, attentive worker, as they were. Successful people are present.

When the meeting's questions have been addressed you will know what you can contribute to the meeting and why you are there. Stay very clearly within your realms of knowledge and you will be able to extract what you need from the meeting and won't be boring or speak outside your real experience.

Positively support any ideas that you agree with from others. That simple generosity will not go unnoticed! It is a very adult reaction and as you probably know a lot of bad business practice is not adult but immature. Disagree with points that you can substantiate but do so with generosity. The best way to do this is to agree with something in the idea. For instance: 'I agree that that point was valid two months ago, but now I don't think it is.' You must be prepared to defend any point.

Stay focused on why you are there and try not to get personal.

As the meeting moves on you might have to change your mind and therefore change your goals.

Second Circle thinking is not rigid so you might find your whole view shifting and this might mean you don't have to voice certain views that you entered the meeting believing. In this way you will stay active, enthusiastic, positive and passionate. These energies will be felt and such qualities are present in all good business practices.

They are the qualities of great success and great humanity.

Ending the Meeting

Like the clarity of a present meeting, we all appreciate a clear ending. We all feel safe when boundaries are clear.

Partings that dither are First Circle and those that are too abrupt are Third Circle. Both leave people confused and unsure. Even an excellent meeting can be muddied by an inept parting.

If you are a leader, your role is very clear and you have to take responsibility for the parting.

- Indicate clearly the meeting is about to be over.

- Sum up.

- Be fair and honest. Will there be another meeting or are you parting without anticipating another meeting?

- If you are on a tight time schedule, be clear about the time allowance early into the meeting.

If you have conducted the meeting in Second Circle the parting will have natural flow. If you have had First or Third energy in the meeting it will be harder to be clear as your attention hasn't been consistent.

A strong, fair parting has these ingredients in it:

- Clearly state the meeting is about to finish and ask if there is anything more to discuss.

- If there is and it is a simple point, address it.

- However, if you are on a tight timetable and a complex point is made, it is fair to say, 'Why wasn't this brought up sooner?' and 'This point has to be dealt with later on another occasion.'

- Say anything negative in a direct, open and uncluttered voice.

- Finish the meeting with a Second Circle physical clarity that says, 'it's over'.

- That could mean you stand up and walk around a desk to shake hands in Second.

- It could mean that you gather papers in Second before standing up to part.

- If it is your room, you can walk people to the door or even the reception area before saying goodbye.

- If it isn't your room, walk in Second to the door, say goodbye and go.

- Be clear in your language as to whether you will be having other encounters.

- If you are not sure, be unsure clearly.

Most misunderstandings in life come from unclear boundaries and an unclear parting can be very confusing.

As a leader you will be dealing with people who will try to manipulate you. Of course being in Second Circle, you will encourage their presence and be able to spot manipulators quickly.

In the parting scenario there are two basic forms of manipulation.

The First Circle ditherer will hesitate and try to prolong the parting to put their final view across. They might even use their victimhood or passive-aggressive tendencies to stay behind and share information withheld from the main meeting.

- You might want their opinion but don't be drawn into a messy parting.

- Be direct, strong and even kind but ask them to formalize their information and leave.

The Third Circle planter can block your way and plant themselves as a seemingly immovable rock. Their point of view is then pronounced forcibly or even loudly.

- Don't be intimidated or rise to Third Circle.

- Be firm and ask them to formalize their view and then, without hesitation, say goodbye and go.

Very soon both First and Third Circle manipulators will realize that being present with you is the only way forward.

As you part in Second, try to say goodbye using names as this will humanize the parting.

Lower Status Parting

This is going to be harder if the leader is not in Second Circle.

It will be very hard to stay present during the meeting but you must work to sustain presence, particularly when those around you are not!

As the meeting draws to a close make sure you have said what you need to say in Second Circle before the end of a meeting.

As soon as the leader indicates the meeting is over, prepare to go. By staying in Second Circle you will quickly realize if the meeting is really over and whether any more business will be done.

If it's definitely over, get up and say goodbye in Second Circle and, if appropriate, shake hands.

On parting, express any positive thought about the meeting to those concerned and if you have a problem or an unexpressed idea, say that you will formalize the idea on request. Leave with good, clear Second Circle energy. This will be dignified and display your full power.

3 Negotiations

In good business practice, when a deal is fairly negotiated and forged then both parties win. If both parties win, then both feel contented and will want to do business with each other again.

This description is one of Second Circle connection and equality: A win-win situation where fairness reigns.

A negotiation where fairness does not reign and no win-win situation exists means that a predator has either pushed the other party into First Circle or duped a Third Circle party by out-bluffing the bluffer. In both cases, the loser feels humiliated.

The predator in this scenario is normally Third Circle and is squashing the other party without fully recognizing their ruthlessness. This is a positive view of the winner giving them the benefit of the doubt.

When you encounter a Third Circle predator you can balance the power and change the negotiation by staying in Second Circle with them. Doing this can actually make them drop their power and you can then observe their true motives. At this point you may choose not to do business with them.

The predator may be in Second Circle. This is a supremely powerful individual and you are probably encountering a highly skilled and successful negotiator. They will generally expect you to fight them in Third Circle or withdraw into First. By deliberately staying in Second Circle you begin to match them and have a clear view of their intentions and ethics. By being present with them you have a choice about whether you want to do business with such an uncompromising partner.

No successful negotiator is in First Circle. If you do meet

one then the chances are they are pretending to be in First but are keenly in Second Circle with a mask of First Circle. Beware of this and don't be beguiled as they will pounce if you drop your guard.

I have outlined generalized points but now the work has to become more specific.

- Before any negotiation, clearly pursue all your needs and points in Second Circle. Prepare these needs.

- Recognize what you want and what would be the best result.

- Recognize what would be the worst result.

- What factors would make a deal and what factors would break the deal?

- Recognize what would make you feel compromised either financially or morally.

- Recognize whether you have more or less power or are equal to the other party.

- Discuss all these recognitions aloud in Second Circle and consequently negotiate with yourself.

This will prepare you and can actually lead you to a position of not wanting to negotiate with a particular party. It might not be worthwhile even to begin.

You in the Power Position

To be in the position of power feels good but before you begin negotiations, be very aware of what you want and what you might concede.

- Do you care about the other party?

- Do you want to work with them further or is this a one-off negotiation?

In a position of power you have only two worries:

1. You may become complacent and drift into First Circle and therefore risk being floored.
2. You could feel so superior that you negotiate in Third and lose your humanity and possibly miss details of the deal, or the deal itself.

- Stay in Second Circle and find out as much as you can about the other party. By staying in Second Circle you will realize the moment you can close the deal but you can also choose to be a benign negotiator in Second and find out potentially powerful information about the other party's point of view.

- Stay present and listen and you will gather information that could mean you don't want to deal with this particular party.

- If you power in with a Third Circle energy or are too casual in First, you can make inappropriate if not disastrous contracts.

- Throughout the negotiation, stay in your Second Circle body, breathe to the other party, listen in your full presence and speak to them.

- Fight the temptation to drift off into First or control them in Third Circle. These reactions can occur throughout the meeting and can only weaken you if you succumb to them.

- Watch them closely and see what Circle they are moving into. Is it fight or flight?

- Try to draw them into Second Circle so that you can see what really is going on. In this way, you will sense the moment to seal the deal or not continue your negotiations.

Actually, although you have power it is harder to stay present if you believe you have that power. You are strangely more vulnerable to losing full attention and being duped.

You in the Less Powerful Position

This is simple. Unless you stay in Second Circle you will not be able to negotiate fully and to your own benefit.

You can forget any successful negotiation if you enter the room in a predisposed defeated First Circle. You will be eaten alive! A First Circle passive-aggressive stance could be perceived as sly and overhumble.

However, most negotiators in a weaker position choose to enter the space in an overenergized, charming or enthusiastic Third Circle: The 'you really need me' approach. This approach has its problems. Many people are turned off by it. It can appear extremely needy and annoying. That is, 'I don't want to do business with this extravagant human being'.

Stay in Second Circle and constantly remind yourself of what you have to offer but don't compromise your position. In this way, like David beating Goliath, you can observe a weakness and conquer it but only if your focus is clear and your aim true.

Remember, the person in power has a contagious energy and you must be alert to stay focused. You might have to consciously breathe low and to the other party, push against a desk to engage yourself, and take time to assess and answer questions. The person in power will assume you will concede and be a pushover. Don't be, but realize that not being a pushover might lead to not getting a deal. If that is the case, then you will probably find the deal was detrimental. In Second Circle you at least can live with yourself.

The best deals are made when both parties are in Second Circle and you can then have the most creative time being adventurous, fair and honest.

4 Selling

All great salesmen are in Second Circle, so if selling is your calling then Second Circle is essential to you.

A First Circle salesperson is a sorry sight as no-one can consistently sell in First Circle. You might earn the occasional sympathetic sale but you have no real selling power in First Circle.

Many competent salesmen are in Third Circle and they might have some success. Most of their success lies in their ability to wear the customer down until the battered customer buys to get rid of the salesperson's intrusive Third Circle energy.

This technique does work on busy or unsophisticated customers but rarely gets people to part with serious money and you are rarely welcomed back for another sales pitch.

The market trader sells a cheap dress very effectively in Third Circle but this technique rarely works when selling an expensive car or house. The trouble with Third Circle selling is it dehumanizes the customer and works on the vulnerable, not on the people who can change your career. The Third Circle salesperson is generally selling to First Circle buyers whose minds they can change, even if the product isn't wanted.

The Second Circle sales pitch is altogether different. At best, it treats the customer as an equal and only wants to sell to those who want the product. At worst, the salesperson can be the most attractive confidence trickster who uses their presence to dupe and steal. I can assure you that all great fraudsters are in Second Circle.

A good salesperson believes, in Second Circle, that their product is great and they have prepared answers, like I have encouraged you to prepare, for all possible negative questions. They have structured their sales pitch in classical form so they can divert from your objections and return to their well-rehearsed pitch. A good salesperson has rehearsed and rehearsed with customers – they know their subject inside out. Their salary depends on how good their presentation skills are so they have to be honed.

Everything in a great salesperson's pitch appears easy and that is how well-rehearsed they are. Hence the saying, 'if someone tells you it's easy they are trying to sell you something.'

On the receiving end, how do you deal with selling techniques? The salesperson will either sell in Third or Second but you, the customer, must be able to foil the salesman if you don't want a product or feel it is overpriced.

Defending Yourself From Great Sellers

A good salesperson can always see the potential customer coming.

You are really tempting in First Circle as you can be easily moulded and controlled. Your lack of attentiveness is a gift to them. You will be signing on the dotted line before you know what you are doing.

The Third Circle customer is also tempting and worth a challenge as your pride and ego can be manipulated.

You will meet a salesperson in one of two ways: either you are on the Salesperson's territory and therefore probably wish to buy what they have on sale; or the salesperson is on your territory, invited or uninvited.

Buying and selling are gladiatorial activities so to survive in Second Circle is essential.

As you walk into a salesperson's territory, be prepared.

- Why are you there?

- Do you want to buy anything?

- What do you want specifically?

- How much are you prepared to pay?

- Have you researched what you should be paying?

If this list seems obvious, that's because it is, but most buyers haven't clearly asked or answered those questions and are therefore bait for the salesperson. Your lack of preparation makes you a ditherer and easily manipulated into buying something you don't want at a price you can't afford.

After you have done your preparation and if you stay in Second Circle you are not a pushover and you will probably find most of the salespeople you meet fade into First Circle – their Third Circle bluff being deflated by your clarity – and you can do an appropriate deal or go somewhere else for a better bargain.

If your presence places you into this powerful position the only question you have to ask yourself is, 'Do I want to buy here again?' If you believe that you cannot do a deal with an individual, leave sooner rather than later.

When the salesperson is on your territory, either office or home, you might feel too safe, which is what most salespersons rely on. You might relax just a bit too much. Fight this tendency to feel at home as it will take you into First Circle.

If you haven't invited the salesperson, deal with them clearly and swiftly. Unless you have a strong interest in their products, do not let them into your space.

The salesperson has won a major victory if you do invite them in, as many people agree to buy a product or arrange another time-wasting meeting just to get them out of their home. This is a known tactic.

If you have an interest in their product, make arrangements for another meeting so you can do all the appropriate research. This will probably be less time-consuming in the long run and will prevent you buying something at an inflated price.

It is accurate to say that if you can engage the salesperson in Second Circle and have them move out of Third Circle you will make a faster decision as to whether you want to do business with them.

If you invite the salesperson into your space then you must do your research before they arrive. This will protect you and save time. So aim to control the proceedings with a direct Second Circle energy.

Lead the pitch by asking the questions you need to ask and not being waylaid by their distractions. A sale can be easy for both parties if the facts are clear. If they are not, don't buy.

Use the fundamental, structured thinking pattern, seek all the information you need and move towards a conclusion which is: 'To buy or not to buy'.

If there is a risk in the purchase, you will reveal it by probing appropriately; if you know the risk you can decide whether you want to take it. If the salesperson doesn't have answers, note whether they are in Second Circle with you. A shift in First or Third Circle might indicate a falsehood.

If you are not comfortable and have no desire to buy, end the meeting directly and cleanly.

Bad salespeople can only make a living because most of us have not done our research and are too casual in their presence.

If a salesperson has a good product and a fair deal and is honest, they will easily move in Second Circle and be clear, direct and open.

Remember, confidence tricksters are real salespeople with nothing to sell and they thrive on the public not being fully present to their tactics. Many legendary tricksters are in Second Circle but they cannot operate if you are in Second Circle with them and have Second Circle knowledge of what you realistically want for your money.

The word realistic is important as the trickster thrives on our unrealistic greed!

5 Interviews

I don't believe you can have a career of any substance without attending an interview or conducting one. Of course I am going to advocate that you are present on both sides. Surprisingly, this often doesn't happen. The person conducting the interview can appear bored or self-satisfied and the interviewee can be too nervous and unable to be present.

If you are on the side of the table which has the power and you are interviewing a candidate, what do you want to achieve and find out? The correct and proper answer is this:

> 'I want to find out the best qualities in the candidate and whether I want to work with them.'

If the above is true, to uncover the candidate's true qualities you must question and work with them in Second Circle and not fall into the commonly found habits that include deliberately withdrawing into First Circle to see how they cope or confronting them in Third Circle to see how resilient they can be.

These tactics might reveal a few strong, no-nonsense candidates but they normally confound the sensitive and you will risk losing sight of an intelligent and instinctive employee. Interviewing in Third Circle could lead you to employ an impressive Third Circle bully.

On the other side of the table, when you are being interviewed, do you really want to work with a First Circle, defeated employer or a bluffing, overenthusiastic or aggressive one? Probably not. You want to be in the company of someone who is good at their job, pro-active and sensitive to the ideas and feelings of others. In other words, a Second Circle work colleague.

You won't recognize who and what your employer might be unless you are fully present in the interview. Without this presence you cannot make an informed choice as to whether you want to work with them.

Second Circle Interviewing Tactics

Interviewer

Always read a CV with full presence. Don't speed-read it but give it your full attention; in this way you will notice anomalies but also understand the strengths and weaknesses of the candidate. List all your positive and negative reactions to the CV. As you work through this process enough you will be able to do it thoroughly and yet quickly.

Meet the candidate at the door, shake hands in Second Circle and see how they respond. Are they in First or Third or can they meet you in Second Circle?

As you observe them, see how frightened they are and whether they can stay connected to you through their fear. This fear can be a positive thing because it means that they care about their performance in the interview and really want to impress you, but the fear shouldn't overwhelm them and make them passive.

- Can they make honest eye contact with you, not withdrawn or too controlling and steely?

- When they speak are they mumbling or too loud or can they speak to you?

- As they sit, do they withdraw or lounge in an overconfident way? Are they too small in the space or are they taking over your space?

- Do they listen and answer your questions appropriately or do they stay on their own track whatever you ask or interrupt you and try to control all your enquiries?

Be very sure of what you want from the interview – not only what you need to find out but what you need to communicate.

Continually be present with the candidate and try to get them into Second Circle. If they refuse to shift out of First or Third Circle, ask detailed questions of Third Circle interviewees and enquire after the personal interests of a First Circle one.

The trouble is, however good they seem, if they cannot respond to you in Second Circle, you haven't really met them and they haven't really listened to you so you can't get a clear view of their true beliefs and potential.

Remember, though, if you have stayed extra present with them then it is a very secretive person who refuses to budge out of First or Third Circle.

Interviewee

Before attending any interview, ask the simple question – 'Do I want the job?' Obviously the answer should be yes, unless you are interviewing just for practice, which many people do. In both cases you should prepare.

- Research the company or institution. Know who works there or has worked there. Who will be on the panel and why could you be of use to the organization?

- Walk into the room, shake hands and sit down in Second Circle.

- Keep breathing and bring into the room your desire to succeed in the interview. So many people don't take this simple directive. Why would anyone want to work with you if you seem casual or arrogant?

- Prepare out loud everything you want to express about yourself and find out about the position.

- Prepare for all the worst questions you might be asked and opinions you might be asked to give. For instance, are there weaknesses in your CV? Prepare what you know your strengths and weaknesses are.

If your preparation is thorough, you will be able to divert from your prepared path, speak off the cuff and comment on any ideas the interviewing panel might supply.

Staying in Second Circle as you are being interviewed is the most powerful statement you can make about your strength of personality and purpose. It will give you plenty of information about them. If they don't shift into Second Circle they will probably turn out to be unsatisfying colleagues. The only problem in staying present when those across the table are not could be that they don't actually want your power and authenticity. That might sound glum but at least you know that if you decide to take the job.

6 Bad News and Good

Conveying Bad News

Here is the simple truth: The more clarity and structure you can create when conveying bad news, the easier it is for the person who has to receive it.

The structure acts as scaffolding that holds the news in a more bearable form. The clarity of structure also ensures that the information is clearly heard. People will not hear bad news if there is any lack of clarity in the presentation.

It is an unenviable task to be the bearer of bad news, but if you have any power in an organization you will, at some point, have to bear unpleasant news.

If you work in certain professions – educational, legal or medical – bearing bad news is a professional necessity and should be done with humanity and in Second Circle.

The fear of bearing bad news often means the messenger performs in a too-casual and messy way, making it much more painful for the receiver.

Let us turn the tables. When you receive bad news there are certain factors that make you feel known and honoured.

You want your dignity respected and you want to be addressed by someone who is present to you and your distress. You want someone who will take your distress and even anger without flinching. You want to be given clear and precise information without verbal padding or mumbling. You want to be treated as a fellow human being with feelings. You want to know the facts and reasons and be allowed to ask questions.

In short, you want the messenger to be in Second Circle

with you, to receive you and your pain and to be as clear as possible with you, honouring your human responses.

To be able to perform as a messenger of bad tidings in the above way makes you a great, responsible and compassionate human being!

Perhaps it is too much to ask to be so super-human but you can try to fulfil some of the criteria of this type of messenger and not be the casual, mumbling First Circle messenger or the insensitive and hard Third Circle messenger.

Here are some Do's and Don'ts of being a good messenger.

- Do have all the facts to hand so you can answer any questions you might be asked.

- Do prepare the clearest, most direct and yet compassionate opening statement.

- Don't pad that statement with sentimental or hesitating language.

- Don't think about yourself; place your concern on the receiver of the news.

- Do make sure the receiver is in Second Circle with you so that they have an optimum chance to hear and understand the news. This will minimize their confusion and your need to repeat yourself.

- Don't mumble and don't push your voice, but breathe and speak to them.

- Don't rush – allow pauses so they can digest the news and appreciate that you are not rushing through the event. Give them time.

- Do schedule a decent amount of time to convey the news.

- Do give them the facts but don't initially overload them. Give them time to ask questions.

- Do try and tell the news in a private and secure place, not one where you can be inappropriately disturbed.

- Do be prepared to take their pain and wrath in Second Circle and recognize their feeling – this will help to comfort them.

- Don't comfort them inappropriately or give them false hope. Be honest.

- If the news is wholly or partly their responsibility, for instance, regarding their laziness at work, explain that and help them to address the problem in the future.

- If the news is not their responsibility, give them information about where they can receive help in the future.

Finish the meeting cleanly and try to make sure they are leaving the space with some safety and guidance.

Care for them and then care for yourself by clearing the experience out of you before moving on to the next task in your day. You have to realize their distress has probably entered your body and you need to remove it before it compounds in you and you take that distress into the rest of your day.

Conveying Good News

This should be a joyous and welcome presentation but you must still be careful and formalize the occasion as you could be so enthusiastic that you give a too-positive message and lead to expectations that are not valid.

Create a clear space to perform the message in, and make

sure you are present and not in a euphoric Third Circle. Make sure your audience is in Second Circle before you give the news. Be direct and clear about the exact boundaries of their good fortune.

They are likely to move into First or Third as they receive the news, but stay clear in your presence to make sure they understand it accurately. If their tendency is to be in Third Circle they might overblow the news and expect more than you are giving. A tendency towards First Circle is likely to underplay the news and you will have to reinforce the positive power of the news.

Conclusion

A book needs a conclusion. But the work on your presentation skills that we have been exploring in this book has no ending, only repeated beginnings. Your work never concludes: you are only as good as your last communication.

To keep your attention focused on this notion of continual work, here are some reminders, designed to keep you in contact with your power and ability to lead in Second Circle.

Remember that voice and presence are not special talents that just a few are born with and are not qualities that cannot be developed.

After many years of teaching, I am convinced that we are all born with presence and remarkable voices. However, many of us have these qualities destroyed or smothered as we grow up. The clear energy of our presence and voices is somehow eroded and with that erosion, there is a loss of your personal power. I have seen thousands of people rediscover their full presence and voice and then go on to develop and strengthen their ability to communicate powerfully. Stay alert to the pressures of the times we live in, and guard against losing your natural abilities by practising your Second Circle presence.

Remember that there are no quick fixes and that you cannot have success without hard and dedicated work.

We are being led to believe something that any educationalist knows to be untrue – that there are shortcuts to success. It is true that you can be lucky and have success and even celebrity without much effort, but this achievement cannot be maintained without sustained working processes. It is short-term and will make your success short-lived. Practise and hard work will bring lasting results.

Remember that we are living in a time when there has been a paucity of good and humane communications.

In line with the quick fix approach, voice and presence work has recently been taught in a cosmetic and superficial way. We can blame this approach on our age-old affair with what is now known as 'spin'. In essence, spin is a form of communication which sounds plausible but has no content. Spin has no desire for a dialogue but has a desire to silence the listener with a shallow flair. We all encounter this type of communication from telephone call centres – the charming or chirpy style that disarms but never serves our needs or seems to care. Spin leaves us feeling controlled and powerless, our humanity unacknowledged. Resist the power of spin in your own communications: care for your audience and they will appreciate your message.

And my final reminder is designed to keep you on your toes. One of the greatest martial artists in the world once said to me, 'Never trust anyone who tells you how to survive or gives you a format of fighting moves. All you can do when you are threatened, Patsy, is stay in the moment and be present.'

The same thought applies to power presentation. You must stay in Second Circle as you prepare and practise. In this way you will realize, on a daily basis, where your working focus should be, on your body, breath or voice. When you are in Second Circle you can mould your content as you present. All important communications have form and are therefore formal, but by being in Second Circle, that formality gains humanity and authenticity. Present with your full power and humanity, and ensure that the work continues.

Prepare, practise and stay present.

Checklist

The Body

- Are you present in your body?
- When you walk into a room are you noticed?
- Do you feel in and connected to your body?

If your answer is 'yes' then you are in good physical order; if 'no' then you have to check the following physical areas.

Are your feet securely on the ground with the weight slightly forward on the balls of your feet?
   Are your knees braced or even pushed back?

- Unlock your knees. Remember any bracing here will distort the whole of your body, breath system and voice.

Is your pelvic area balanced above your legs and aligned to support your spine? If not, then your pelvic area is either thrust forward or pushed back.

- Re-centre this crucial area by flopping over from the waist and coming up through the whole body without distortion through your pelvis. If this area is held or braced then you have no chance to breathe or support your power.

Now the check goes into your spine – the placing of your spine is so important to your whole image. If the spine is contorted you are sending powerful signals to the world about your presence, as well as rendering your breath and voice presence-less! Is your spine slumped or braced up?

- Regulate the position and alignment of the spine.

Is your upper chest lifted up or depressed?

- Place your hand on your sternum and position the sternum without these tensions.

Shoulders – are they lifted, pulled back or rounded forward?

- Release your shoulders until you feel that they hang freely without you controlling them.

Is your head on top of your spine, or pulled back, tucked down or pushed forward?

- Balance your head on the top of the spine without any pressure being felt at the back of the neck, a crunching feeling, or any locking in the throat.

Is your jaw clenched?

- Unlock it, so that the lips are together but without clenching the teeth or blocking the back of the throat.

How do you walk? Do you scuff the floor, looking down and moving without urgency? Do you strut, making too much noise with your feet and pushing your body through space with effort?

- Walk with urgency but ease and when you stop, keep that energy within you.

How do you sit? Slumped and depressed? Braced and held?

- Sit with your spine up but not locked.

Quick Body Warm-Up

- Lie on your back with your calves supported by a chair, head supported by a small cushion. Feel your spine supported by the floor.
- Your jaw should be relaxed, shoulders open and arms by your sides.
- Try not to lift your sternum as you breathe.
- Feel the release around your thighs , opening your pelvic area and locked stomach muscles.
- Hold this position for at least ten minutes.
- Roll over on to your side, rest, then roll on to your hands and knees and slowly come up, feet on the ground and rolling up through the spine, head last of all.
- Let the shoulders fall into place. They should feel heavy and open.
- Lift your spine into place by remembering how it felt on the floor. It should not be rigid and arched or slumped.
- Repeat the same process with the pelvic area.
- Notice that the knees aren't locked.
- Let your weight flop the body over until your torso is hanging freely from the waist.
- Allow your head to fall on your chest and feel its weight.
- Shake the shoulders and allow the back of the neck and jaw to release.
- Slowly roll up again and see if your alignment is different, shoulders released and spine up.
- Look around the room and focus your energy on

something outside yourself, like a picture or a tree through the window.

- Next, walk with energy. Imagine you have somewhere to go and are moving directly but without force. Feel a new energy engage in you and a gear change in your physical state.
- When you feel this shift stop walking but allow your body to keep moving forward – stay on the balls of your feet and don't move back or settle by either locking your knees, pulling down or bracing up in your spine or interfering in the placing of your shoulders.
- Now go to a wall and place both hands on it as though you were going to gently but firmly push the wall over. Your feet must be on the ground, weight on the balls, knees unlocked, spine up, strong, but not rigid, shoulders released so that you can feel energy and breath low in the pelvic area.
- Breathe in this position. Stay connected to the wall, don't feel you are pulling the wall's energy into you or that you are forcing your upper body's power into the wall, just push with strong but efficient energy.
- When you feel this energy, move away from the wall, allowing the contact with the wall to place you into the room with your full physical presence.

Breath

Do you breathe on a fluid and regular rhythm, in and out?

- Try to really feel yourself taking oxygen in and out – this essential life-force.

Does your upper chest lift as you breathe?

- Keep it still.

Do your shoulders interfere with the breath, lift, pull back or brace?

- Unlock your shoulders as you breathe.

Can you feel the ribcage open?

- Open the ribcage around the sides and back.

Can you feel a hold in the lower abdominal area?

- Allow the breath to go as low as it can.

Do you rush the intake of breath, pull in the breath or over-control the breath?

- Concentrate your thoughts on feeling the fine readiness of your breath.

Even when you feel the readiness of your breath, do you want to go before you're ready, hold before you go or deflate the breath?

- Speak only on the readiness of the breath.

Do you go beyond your natural supported breath?

- Take breath when you need it.

Do you take breath before you need it?

- Go beyond that need.

- Breathe as you think, listen and speak.
- Keep the movement of breath fluid and take your power as you breathe.

Do you overbreathe a room? Do you underbreathe a room?

- Breathe the room.

Do you breathe beyond the person you are addressing or barely to them?

- Breathe to them.

Quick Breath Warm-Up

- Lie on your back with your calf muscles resting on a chair, head supported by a small cushion.
- Place one hand on your upper chest and one on your stomach.
- Keep the shoulders, neck, jaw and thighs released.
- For several minutes do nothing but breathe in and out, slowing down the rhythm to its simplest and slowest, breathing silently.
- After several minutes lay your hands by your sides.
- Keeping the breath slow and silent, check in on its state. If you encounter tension, remind that tension it can go!
- Starting with the jaw, take a mental journey through your body. Visit the shoulders and upper chest. Remind the shoulderblades to open and use the floor for support.
- Feel your spine, buttocks and pelvic area supported by the floor and the stomach muscles released.
- Some sections of the body will fail to open – stop breathing as you meet those areas. However, try to keep the breath fluid in and out.

- Now place your hands around the centre of your body and find your ribcage. Feel the sides of the ribcage and feel any movement of breath and then slide your hands back to feel the movement in the back of the ribcage. On the inward breath the ribcage opens around the centre of your torso, without the shoulders or upper chest lifting. After the ribs move out and up, muscles in the stomach, abdominal area and pelvis release and move out. On the outward breath all these muscles move in and create a column of air that will support your power and sound and consequently send that energy into the world.
- Now interchange the breath through the nose and mouth. The nose breath is calmer but you will also need the mouth.
- As you lie there breathing, begin to identify the moment of readiness. Take time to investigate this moment and when you feel this readiness, breathe in, feel the suspension and readiness of the breath and then breathe out using the ribcage and abdominal muscles to support an 's' sound.
- After a few releases you should feel the breath is in contact with the 's' sound. This breath contact or connection is called support.
- Take time and enjoy the ease and simplicity of this release.
- As soon as you have experienced the support on the intake of breath, concentrate on the release.
- As the breath supports the 's' there is a moment when you know you should take another breath.
- Spend a few minutes breathing with that clarity, responding to your body's needs.
- You can extend and feel this release more sensually if you change the sound to a 'z' and then gently pull your knees towards you with your hands. After several releases in this position you should be feeling breath connection and

support clearly. Replace your legs on to the chair and return to a silent and calm breath.

- Remove your legs from the chair and roll on to your side.
- Lie there and enjoy the release around your shoulders and neck, and feel the heaviness of your arms.
- Feel the breath around your body.
- Move on to your hands and knees and allow your bottom to collapse on to the calf muscles, your forehead to rest on the floor, and your arms to rest on the floor above your head.
- Release your shoulders and neck.
- As you breathe in this position (called the child position in yoga) your back will naturally open and you will feel the abdominal muscles, although restricted by your thighs, actively engage.
- In this position you can clearly sense the readiness of your breath.
- After taking a few breaths here, slowly sit back on your feet, place the spine up, and allow the shoulders to release. You will now feel the breath go down deeply into your lower abdominal power base. Place a hand there and release on a 'z' from this low support.
- Start to contact your full breath power.
- Now, get to your feet, coming up carefully. As you stand, check the position of your feet on the floor, with the weight forward and the feet hip-width apart.
- Look around you and focus on an object across the room to bring you back into Second Circle.
- Place your concentration on your breathing – hopefully it feels calmer and is moving deeper into the body.
- Walk over to a wall and gently push against it. Notice as you push whether the breath is low and connected in your body.

- While pushing, release on a 'z' and see if you can identify the breath's power.
- You can also feel this connection by holding a chair above your head and breathing and then releasing on 'z'.
- After coming away from the wall or putting the chair down, maintain that connection with your breath – don't return to old habits.
- Repeat until you stay connected. After being connected you will be able to switch this connection on at will.
- Now try walking with purpose, keeping the breath free, and when you stop, avoid going backwards in your body or deflating or holding or locking the breath. This practice can be done anywhere. You can walk in the street, then stop and check that your body and breath are connected and are present in you.

Voice

Is your voice free? Or do you feel it in your throat? Do you push it or do you 'undervoice'?

- Open your voice and keep it full and not forced or pushed.
- Feel the freedom on intoning into speaking.

Do you push down on your voice? Do you pull it back into your mouth and throat?

- Place your voice forward.
- Commit to an open 'ooh' and send your voice out.

Does your voice fall back or do you push it out?

- Aim to reach a target, not push beyond it or fall short.

Do you feel your voice is dull or stuck?

- Move your voice freely through your range with ease and enjoyment.

Do you feel your voice is thin or stuck in one quality?

- Warm up all the resonances and use them as you speak.

Quick Voice Warm-Up

- Sit on a chair, spine straight, shoulders released and upper chest open, feet on the floor with a concentration of energy forward on the balls of your feet.
- Breathe low and calmly, identifying the moments when the breath is suspended and ready.
- Imagine that you are about to speak and see what reactions are triggered in your throat, jaw, face or tongue. The expectancy of speech is often enough to reveal key tensions. Try to recognize even the slightest blockages or tics of tension.
- Now imagine having to speak to the person you most fear. This will expose your tensions more vividly.
- Now imagine the best listener you have ever had in your life present in the room and examine whether any tensions fall away from you. When you discover an ease, stay with it and, remembering to breathe, perform the next series of exercises.
- Gently massage your face. Pay particular attention to the jaw and between your eyes. After the massage, check if your face feels different.
- Gently massage the back of your neck and then, extremely gently, your whole neck. Feel the larynx and massage

around it very carefully. Massage up under your chin and begin to release the back of your tongue through the underbelly of your chin.

- Look into a mirror and see if you look different.
- Now re-place any tensions in the face, jaw or tongue that you know are part of any of your blocked energies.
- Using a mirror as a constant check, move through the next series of exercises.
- Bunch up all the facial muscles and then allow them to release without re-placing the habits. As soon as you feel the need to re-place any tension you have gone back to your habits. Even if you can't feel these tensions you will see your habit in action in the mirror. Do this at least three times.
- Push your lips forward and then pull them back into a grimace. Repeat three times.
- Open your mouth as wide as possible, followed by a release. Repeat three times.
- Stretch your tongue by placing it outside your mouth, trying to keep it parallel to the floor. Repeat three times.
- On and with the breath, begin to gently hum.
- Keep breathing and if the voice tightens as you hum, check all the areas of tension until you can maintain a gentle but sustained hum without tension. Hum until you feel that the voice motors smoothly and can be sustained.
- When the voice feels warmed, stand up and walk with energy until you really feel in your Second Circle body.
- Pick up a reading and stand side on to a wall.
- Place one hand against the wall and push gently until you feel your breath engage.
- Read aloud with this push in place, all the time monitoring your tensions and, if necessary, stopping to release them.

- After reading aloud a 90-second section, come away from the wall and read the same section again. The voice should be freer.

Speech

Do you feel words are not fully in your mouth but falling back?

- Aim to finish every word with need.

Are you over-articulating and dwelling on words inappropriately?

- Speak clearly but move the words forward with a need to communicate.

Are your words sloppy?

- Fully articulate them and give them weight.

Are your vowels diminished?

- Use them to move you and your voice forward.

Are you connected to the words?

- Experience what you say as you say it.

Quick Speech Warm-Up

- Open your mouth so that the speech muscles can work.
- Massage the face and gently pull open the jaw.

- Smile and open the jaw without overstretching it and then allow the lips to come together easily and without clenching the teeth.
- Move your tongue around this space, top, bottom and side to side.
- Feel the back of your front teeth.
- Feel the ridge behind the front teeth.
- Tap your tongue on this ridge.
- Notice any difference in the mouth space and the tongue's relationship to that space.
- Extend your lips forward and vocalize an 'ooh', keeping the jaw released.
- Move 'ooh' into 'moo'.
- Now sound out the following consonants and words:
  - M, N, W, L, D, B, V, G
  - P, T, K, F
  - M M M M B B B B P P P P: Come – Dream – Rub – Scrub – Pop – Drop
  - W W W W W W: Water – Wag – Woe
  - D D D D T T T T: Dead – Said – But – Tight – Might
  - TH TH TH TH
  - Birth – Death – Mirth
  - L L L L: Lily
  - F F F F V V V V: Have – Give – Love – Puff – Tough – Off
  - G G G G K K K K: Spark – Dark – Mark – God – Long – Song – Log
  - ING: Laughing – Singing – Walking – Eating
  - M – N – NG
  - L: Call – Wall – Dwell – Bell
  - R R R R: Right – Round – Romp
  - S S S S Z Z Z Z: Birds – Herds – Shirts – Pumps – Tights

- Go to a wall and gently push against it with one hand.
- Stay breathing and centred.
- Focus in Second Circle to a point just above the eyeline.
- Release an 'ooh' to place your voice.
- Now breathe and mouth a piece of text without using any voice, but feel all the muscles working to form every sound.
- Be particularly diligent when mouthing ends of words and multisyllabic words.
- When you finish mouthing your extract, go back and read it in full voice.
- Now just speak the vowels of your piece on full voice.
- On finishing this exercise, go back immediately and put in the consonants.
- You will be speaking so clearly and fully!

Pace

Do you speak too quickly?

- Make sure you physically speak each word fully and imagine the words' meaning as you speak it.

Do you speak too slowly?

- Know that you must have an urgent need to speak to keep a story engaging and as long as you physically connect to every word you will not be speaking too fast.

Rhythm

Is your rhythm pessimistic – does it fall?

- Work with the returning energy of the heartbeat, the iambic, to launch you into optimism.

Is your rhythm too controlled and locking off your emotional life?

- Don't pause as you speak but allow the power of your words to move you and your rhythm forward.

Listening

Do you disconnect as you listen?

- Work at staying present.

Do you want to interrupt as you listen?

- Stay present and don't presume you know what is going to be said.

Listening Tips

- On a regular basis, practise trying to experience silence.
- In silence, lie on the floor or sit upright and pick out sounds around you.
- When you are accustomed to this silence, play some favourite music on a low volume. Your ears will stretch towards the sound, heightening your listening.
- Notice how you listen to people that interest you. Really appreciate what they are saying.
- Check that your listening doesn't wander off into First or Third Circle
- Practise listening attentively to those who annoy you, don't respect you or feel superior to you.
- This will be a huge struggle but you will learn a lot about yourself and those around you.

Structure

Do you get lost as you speak?

- Plan your intellectual journey, thoroughly.

Do you know what your journey is so clearly that you can't be bothered to take anyone on it?

- Take people along with you. Tell them a story and bit by bit reveal your message.

Tips on Structure

When you write a speech or plan a presentation you should start with scaffolding your ideas.

- Where do I start? How do I open the debate?
- What points should be cited and explored?
- Where am I going?
- What is my resolve?

Try this exercise.

- Describe a known but complex actual journey. It could be your journey to work every day or the one you take to visit a parent or friend.
- Speak it aloud.
- Describe it clearly and thoroughly and as though the person hearing the directions must take this journey now and urgently.
- Now describe the same journey in a more relaxed way, making it as colourful as you can. You are still

structuring your journey but making it more personal and interesting.

- Imagine you are defending a close friend wrongly accused of a minor crime. You weren't with them at the time of the crime but have five concrete reasons why they couldn't have committed it.
- At this stage, don't be personal or emotional. Explain the facts clearly and conclude with a reason why they are not guilty.
- Now flesh this defence with any personal or passionate details as you defend your friend.
- Now go to a problem that you face in your workplace: a problem you know how to solve, even if no-one has asked you to solve it.
- Start with speaking the problem and then list all the factors of the problem, describing the solutions and concluding with the action that should immediately be taken.
- Imagine, in this preparation, all the objections your colleagues will raise and make sure you have information to defend your point of view.

These checks are simple but vital in your working process. As you identify your strengths and weaknesses you will be able to hone and improve your skills. Most great professional speakers know that they have to work every day on their craft and constantly improve it by conscious work and checks. You have all the practical skills to begin real preparation for all the communication challenges you will inevitably meet.

Recommended Reading

Read aloud from any of the following to improve your presentation and speaking skills, using the exercises throughout the book:

- *The Penguin Book of Twentieth Century Speeches* edited by Brian MacArthur

- The opening of any Charles Dickens novel

- Any Shakespearean monologue

- John Donne's 'Sermons'

- 'A Modest Proposal' by Jonathan Swift (probably the finest satirical essay in the English language)

These suggestions are all designed to be challenging – I am deliberately setting the bar high, not only to develop the physical strength of your voice, but also to give muscle to your work on structure.

PATSY RODENBURG

PRESENCE: HOW TO USE POSITIVE ENERGY FOR SUCCESS

This book will transform you.
It will invigorate every aspect of your life.
It will awaken, within, your full potential.

By revealing the three circles of energy inside all of us, Patsy Rodenburg will change how you engage with others: how you look, listen, think, feel, learn and do business. It will teach you how to be more present in every aspect of your life.

o   Learn how correct breathing is crucial to communication

o   Discover how to be more aware of your surroundings

o   Make the most of every situation and opportunity

o   Use positive energy to take charge

We all want to live life to the full.
Allow *Presence* to help you achieve that goal.

'I am an enormous fan of her work. What is wonderful about her is her directness and clarity of teaching and her enthusiasm' Dame Judi Dench